AS IF

Before you start to read this book, take this moment to think about making a donation to punctum books, an independent non-profit press,

@ https://punctumbooks.com/support/

If you're reading the e-book, you can click on the image below to go directly to our donations site. Any amount, no matter the size, is appreciated and will help us to keep our ship of fools afloat. Contributions from dedicated readers will also help us to keep our commons open and to cultivate new work that can't find a welcoming port elsewhere. Our adventure is not possible without your support.
Vive la open-access.

Fig. 1. Hieronymus Bosch, *Ship of Fools* (1490–1500)

ESSAYS IN *AS YOU LIKE IT*

William N. West

Dead Letter Office
BABEL Working Group

AS IF: ESSAYS IN *AS YOU LIKE IT*. Copyright © 2016 William N. West. This work carries a Creative Commons BY-NC-SA 4.0 International license, which means that you are free to copy and redistribute the material in any medium or format, and you may also remix, transform, and build upon the material, as long as you clearly attribute the work to the authors and editors (but not in a way that suggests the authors or punctum books endorses you and your work), you do not use this work for commercial gain in any form whatsoever, and that for any remixing and transformation, you distribute your rebuild under the same license. http://creativecommons.org/licenses/by-nc-sa/4.0/

First published in 2016 by
Dead Letter Office, BABEL Working Group
A division of punctum books
Earth, Milky Way
www.punctumbooks.com

The BABEL Working Group is a collective and desiring-assemblage of scholar-gypsies with no leaders or followers, no top and no bottom, and only a middle. BABEL roams and stalks the ruins of the posthistorical university as a multiplicity, a pack, looking for other roaming packs with which to cohabit and build temporary shelters for intellectual vagabonds. We also take in strays.

ISBN-13: 978-0615988177
ISBN-10: 0615988172
Library of Congress Cataloging Data is available from the Library of Congress

Book design: Kristen McCants & Vincent W.J. van Gerven Oei
Cover image: William Blake, *Jaques and the Wounded Stag* (1806)

Contents

FOREWORD ◆ Trying	ix
INTRODUCTION ◆ *As You Like It*	15
1 ◆ What happens in *As You Like It*?	19
2 ◆ What is the play about?	25
3 ◆ What's in a name?	33
4 ◆ What happens when Rosalind dresses as a boy?	39
5 ◆ Where is Arden?	45
6 ◆ Why do we hear about what Jaques said to a deer?	53
7 ◆ What does Jaques telling us about Touchstone telling time tell us about them?	59
8 ◆ What is pastoral?	63
9 ◆ What does Jaques mean when he says, "All the world's a stage"?	69
10 ◆ Why does Touchstone say the truest poetry is the most faining? Or is it "feigning"?	77
11 ◆ What happens when Ganymede dresses as a girl?	83
12 ◆ What is love?	89
13 ◆ What is the virtue in "if"?	97
14 ◆ What happens in the epilogue?	101
15 ◆ The end?	107
Notes to the Text	111
Works Cited	121

FOREWORD

Trying

Not long ago I was invited to write a *vade mecum* into Arden, in the form of a guide to Shakespeare's *As You Like It*. It was to be part of a series of short introductions to some of Shakespeare's plays and other widely-read works of literature, aimed at readers, playgoers, actors, students, and aficionados rather than at academics. What appealed to me most about the invitation was the opportunity to write towards a different kind of reader than I usually do and in a different way than I usually do. I liked the idea of trying to say something about a play like *As You Like It* as a whole, in a single gesture, to introduce and conclude in one movement. It would be like, I thought, a lecture, in which you can launch a ninety-minute sortie into a play or a handful of poems, urging a sense of the forest by examining some of its trees. Like a lecture, I thought, the task of writing a guide to *As You Like It* would let me move fast and wander wide; as in a lecture, what I might claim would need to stand for the most part on its own. My arguments and observations would rest on their own persuasiveness, less on citations or the bubble reputation or other kinds of authority. The format of the series called for me to ask a set of broad questions and then to open some answers, a little like leading a seminar, but for one voice. I would get to try to make readers entertain the notions I raised as if they were theirs, even if just for a moment. The book would make pictures of the whole play in single takes, aiming neither for narrow conclusivity nor comprehensiveness, but maybe instead for something like representivity or even suggestiveness. It might not be solidly buttressed with sources like a journal article, but it might be able to go further out on limbs. I took up the project as a challenge.

It *was* a challenge. It was hard not to fall back on all the inertia of scholarly habit, hard to resist the security of offloading references onto other writers who had treated things more fully or masterfully. It was hard to put ideas up for grabs and to try for the flexible back-and-forth of conversation, hard to keep that feel of shared testing of possibilities and the startling responsiveness of interlocutors. Drafts, messages, and phone calls passed back and forth between the commissioning editor and me: one part was too theoretical, another too lodged in historical contexts, another too single-minded in advancing its own claims or too blinkered about how other readers and writers had framed something before. And in the end, despite our attempts to find shared ground, the commissioning editor finally didn't think what I had written fit into the series, and I didn't want to try to make it fit in better than it did. I liked where the project had pushed me and I liked what I had done with it. I liked what I had said, even though what I had written was recognizably not an academic monograph or scholarly article. That it wasn't, and that I couldn't imagine it becoming one, was part of what I liked about it. I didn't know what to do with it, but I knew I didn't want to bury it. And so I sent it to the Dead Letter Office at punctum books.

What I had ended up writing as I tried to emulate talking, I now think, was an example of what Roland Barthes called "the ambiguous genre where the writing vies with the analysis," an *essay*. I don't mean this, obviously, in the sense that as teachers we regularly assign what we call essays to our students and regularly write them. An essay, as assigners almost ritualistically remind other readers and writers, is both an attempt and a testing, a trial of invention and judgment that follows through on a line of thought. Stripped of the security of footnotes and pressed to write concisely to the point, I ended up stumbling onto these demands seriously and in all their distinct rigor. As a particular form of writing, the essay takes its name from Montaigne's famous attempts, although he traced its attentive, meandering shape back to writings by Seneca and Plutarch, as well as the drift of his own musings and conversations. But the impulse to essay may be said to take its cue from a question Montaigne asks, *Que sçay-je?*, "what do I know?" The phrase appears only once in the text of his *Essais,* when he notes that he bears it, with the image of a balance, as his device. Montaigne may have had a medal made of this emblem during the years he was writing his earliest essays, so perhaps he means literally that he carried his question with him. It isn't hard to imagine him handling it as he wrote in his library, as a kind of all-but-unuttered subtext to his writing. In the essay as printed in 1588, Montaigne follows *Que sçay-je?* with *Voylà!,* as if holding the medal up and asking the reader to take a look. Later, annotating his own copy of the printed book, he strikes *Voylà!* through, and the imagined medal recedes into language.

Montaigne's leading question was his version of the skeptical assertions of doubt that were among the aphorisms written in Greek and Latin on the rafters of his library. It might also respond to Aristotle's statement in *Metaphysics* that philosophy begins in wonder and unknowing. But where Aristotle's man who wonders and does not know something works to bring himself from ignorance to knowledge, Montaigne refuses even to be sure of his ignorance and insists on asking. Not knowing is better grasped, Montaigne says, by asking than by asserting. *Que sçay-je?* The question presents a picture in which knowing and not-knowing are less neatly separated, certainly less likely to be opposite. Anyone who asks it is pushed to explore the edges and depths of his or her ignorance, and also to account for what he or she does know. The essay in this tradition is a detailing of one's ignorance, and one's knowledge, in their shadowy and shifting irregularity. It does not look for a one-way flight from unknowing; it tries to sound out the messy contours of beliefs, assumptions, curiosities, and blind spots. Theodor

Adorno observes that "in the emphatic essay thought divests itself of the traditional idea of truth." By a traditional idea of truth Adorno seems to mean something like being objectively right. But neither does the essay, Adorno insists, merely express an idiosyncratic perspective, however carefully. It adumbrates things which only become visible from particular perspectives, in parts and fleetingly. Without becoming fictional or fantastic, an essay tries to follow the limits of traditional ideas of truth and to illuminate other ways of being truthful.

An essay in this trying tradition lays out lines of thought that are not exhaustive. It extends its feeling of wonder not to everything and not systematically, but adventitiously to anything and as fully as it can according to whatever traces it discovers as it goes. An essay, as Adorno also noted, is uninterested in reaching after universals, origins, or absolutes. It engages contingencies. It may be erudite, or not, but not encyclopedic. It begins wherever it is, taking up whatever text or context it finds itself engaged with, and any truths it coins depend on those accidents and happenstances; it "cunningly anchors itself in texts as though they were simply there and had authority." Released from the demand to secure its starting points, taking other bearings, it is freed to seek other headings than other kinds of writing. It follows its texts and contexts where they lead. It responds to each eventuality it addresses wholeheartedly, as if whatever question it asked were all there were to answer, but unlike a conventional scholars' treatment of a problem, it makes no pledge of completeness, either of its treatment or of its topic.

Kenneth Burke's *Language as Symbolic Action* or Northrop Frye's *Anatomy of Criticism,* both of which are subtitled *essays,* perhaps really do try to explain everything on the basis of the questions they ask, as if each offered readers a kind of literary Theory of Everything. The vivid, inset images of Jacob Burckhardt's flickeringly evocative *Culture of the Renaissance in Italy,* which also calls itself an essay, read as more designedly fragmented, and essays like Montaigne's or Barthes's are more obviously fugitive still. In each of these essays or collections of essays (the difficulty in telling the difference is itself telling), conclusions are offered only through what is provisional and opportunistic. Essaying in this vein doesn't require setting limits between questions, but loosening them. Essaying, it is hard to predict how thought will need to turn as it follows its own course, what unanticipated questions will be raised in the following out of others, what will be included as it proceeds, because it does not work within a field determined ahead of time. Problem and response alike flash up in moments of uncertainty. One realization I came to in my essaying is that Shakespeare's *As You Like It* may itself be approached as a collection of essays enacted by its characters, a group of experiments that test how the world might be other than it is. The play — and could "play" itself translate "essay"? — is in a way its own guide to the essay and its applications.

My essay on *As You Like It,* if that is what it is, touches on much that is basic, much that is familiar or commonplace, in part because of the circumstances in which it was written, but in part, too, because some of those familiar questions seem to me the ones I most wanted to answer about this play and the kind of problem that eluded the writing I undertake more often. I was able to ask them because I tried to write as if *As You Like It* were simply there and had authority. My essay does not try to say everything about *As You Like It,* but rather to take up the questions it does engage as if each in turn was what most demanded to be answered. It does not make a claim to comprehensiveness or conclusiveness, as a commentary or a monograph could, maybe even should. It is a guide to *As You Like It,* but like any reader I acknowledge that there are other ways in.

Summers 2013, 2014, 2015   — W. N. W.
Weekapaug

INTRODUCTION

As You Like It

If we were obliged to answer the question which of Shakespeare's plays contains, not indeed the fullest picture of his mind, but the truest expression of his nature and habitual temper, unaffected by special causes of exhilaration or gloom, I should be disposed to choose *As You Like It*.
— A.C. Bradley, *Oxford Lectures on Poetry* (1909)

As You Like It is and long has been one of Shakespeare's best-loved plays. Critics in the nineteenth century in particular were captivated by what they saw as its artful blend of wistful nostalgia, buoyant optimism, and a dash of worldly wisdom in what the great Romantic essayist William Hazlitt declared "the most ideal of any of this author's plays." Love for the play was tied up in an equally ardent Victorian love for the character of Rosalind, which even Shakespeare's most famous baiter George Bernard Shaw recognized with some exasperation: "Who ever failed, or could fail, as Rosalind?"

The play continues to be well-loved by audiences and readers. Less so by the last generation of scholars. Playing on the play's title, the scholar of performance Bruce Smith observes that "[c]uriously, many academic critics since the 1970s... *don't* like it." Important engagements with Rosalind's multiple transvestite disguises, looking at female agency and gender identity, have enriched existing views of Rosalind's intelligence, creativity, and appeal, confirming her in new ways as "the philosopher of the play" and not just its protagonist. But the play was largely bypassed by New Historicists and other avowedly politically and socially engaged trends in scholarship that rose to prominence in the latter half of the twentieth century. These tended to seek out the darker, more obviously fraught comedies, *Twelfth Night* or *A Midsummer Night's Dream,* in their investigations of the cultural poetics of Elizabethan England. Despite the play's clear interest in many of the positions that also interested these critics, like the instability of norms of gender and desire, or the machinations and blind spots of power, *As You Like It* seemed too chipper, too sanguine, too conservative in its conclusion. Smith shares the ideological convictions of such critics (as do I), but suggests that they "have refused to be taken in by the sights and sounds of *As You Like It*" — by all, in fact, that is most *likable* in the play, rather than intelligible or arguable.

As You Like It is indeed astoundingly rich in humor, vigor, and an attractive physicality both displayed and described. I would add that misliking critics, by focusing on an outcome rather than on how the play reaches it, also miss some of the force of the play's lyrical and clever use of language, imaginative flights, and evocative setting to carry an audience or a reader away, as it seems to have done to Hazlitt and even the reluctant Shaw. Yet even at its zenith, praise for *As You Like It* can feel temperate, partly because the play itself seems to be about finding the proper temper for passion and reflection, ecstasies and contemplation. Bradley, for instance, especially admires how precisely *As You Like It* reins in the extremes of Shakespeare's imagination. "[E]xhilaration or gloom" we might find in *Romeo and Juliet, A Midsummer Night's Dream,* or *King Lear*; *As You Like It* can feel much more safely domesticated.

These disparate reactions can be traced to what seems to me a misunderstanding of *As You Like It* as a carefully measured, even reticent, play. In some ways it certainly is, as Smith's disgruntled scholars noticed. It questions deeply-held convictions about property, or knowledge, or desire, or freedom, and imagines compelling alternatives to the world as it is, but then often seems in the end to fall back into conventional positions: Rosalind-Ganymede is really a girl, suitable for Orlando to desire and to marry, but not for Phoebe — or for Celia; Oliver and Celia can happily settle on Corin's homestead because they have the money to do it; the exiled Duke can command his followers to pretend to be his equals in Arden, until of course it is time to return to court. Smith rightly notes that the pleasure in the course of the play need not impeach our sense that its conclusions may not be ours. But its very modesty allows *As You Like It* to experiment with a kind of radical foundation-shaking that is rarely found in Shakespeare or elsewhere.

The optimism of *As You Like It*, beginning, middle, and end, comes from its relentless attention to how *what may be* need not be mired in *what is*. The play drives forward, even in the last lines of its epilogue, towards future ways of life that are not merely different but can be *made* different, and made *better,* than present ones. The temperate solutions with which the play concludes are not offered as final, but as clearly open to ongoing changes. The play's very reserve and moderation, its resistance to extremity and desperation and finality, is what allows for its relentless confidence that things can be changed. In this, it is perhaps more literally progressive (that is, *stepping ahead*) and more literally radical (that is, *from the root*) than any settled position on the instabilities of gender, or the elusiveness of equality, or the variety of desire, could be. As Jaques reports Touchstone observing,

"Thus we may see," quoth he, "how the world wags:
'Tis but an hour ago since it was nine,
And after one hour more 'twill be eleven,
And so from hour to hour we ripe and ripe,
And then from hour to hour we rot and rot,
And thereby hangs a tale." (2.7.23–28)

"Rot" sounds much more final, and much more like Jaques than like Touchstone; "ripe" sounds closer to the comic arc of the play. But across the two claims together, there is another, larger claim: everything changes, all the time, and those changes can always be potentially consequential. Thereby hangs the world's tale, always spinning out. It is also true, as the great director Peter Brook said of a 1953 production designed by Salvador Dalí, that "*As You Like It* seems written purely to please." In our pleasures, the play leads us to wag along with the rest of the world, according to the rhythms we can at least in part discern and choose to follow or reject. There is no last step.

1

What happens in As You Like It?

Actually, a lot: a younger brother, badly raised by his older brother after their father's death, rebels; so does another younger brother, who usurps the duchy of his older brother, who in turn flees with his followers to a nearby forest; four pairs of characters meet and part and couple and marry; and besides that, there are combats, ambushes, changes of heart, narrow escapes, and secret plans. But as August Schlegel, a contemporary of Goethe and one of Shakespeare's great translators, observed, "It would be difficult to bring the contents within the compass of an ordinary relation: nothing takes place, or rather what takes place is not so essential as what is said." The events of the plot in *As You Like It* are not really what make up the play. Instead, they are there to create a background against which the characters can reflect on their situations, in love, in society, in family. Jaques's meditations on the world and the stage, or Orlando's poetizing on love, are as much part of the action as Orlando's wrestling match or Rosalind's disguises. The most memorable and central parts of *As You Like It* do not really *happen* at all, or at least not as we usually imagine events or action to happen. They are topics for debate. The hardest work in the play is accomplished not in action, but in words; when Orlando throws Charles to the ground and has to flee the court, the most overt kinds of physical action are left behind with the bruised wrestler.

What really happens in *As You Like It* is talking, thinking, wondering, analyzing, interpreting, discussing what has just happened, what is that like, what to do next, what it all means. *As You Like It* is a play in love with its own voices. Talking and thinking structure the play as much as any events it portrays. Conversations follow their own rhythms, begin, are dropped, then taken up again, informed by new events or considerations — and with every shift, as Rosalind says to Orlando about differences of opinion, "there begins new matter" (4.1.74). Characters return to themes introduced earlier by other characters or develop new viewpoints based on what they say or hear. Few problems are resolved by talking about them, but talking makes their contours clearer, both their consequences and the opportunities they present. In conversation characters practice imagining worlds different from the one they inhabit, and taking steps to make those worlds real.

Act I

Before the play begins, the younger brother of the Duke has overthrown his brother and sent him into exile. The exiled Duke now lives with his companions in the nearby forest of Arden.

A younger son of an aristocratic family, Orlando, complains to his family's aged servant, Adam, that his oldest brother and the head of the family, Oliver, has raised him in neglect. When Oliver appears, Orlando explodes, threatening him and demanding whatever inheritance he has from their father. Oliver expels Orlando from the household, and with him discharges old Adam.

A professional wrestler from the court, Charles, warns Oliver that Orlando is planning to challenge Charles during an exhibition match. Charles is afraid that he may injure Orlando and wants Oliver to talk Orlando out of it. Oliver, though, tells Charles that he doesn't mind if Orlando is hurt or even killed. Charles, no fool, promises that he'll make sure that Orlando is at least maimed. But the next day at the match, to everyone's astonishment, Orlando overthrows Charles so forcefully that it is Charles who is injured. A notable member of the audience, Rosalind, the daughter of the recently exiled Duke who has stayed on at court, tells Orlando that he has overthrown more than his enemies. She and Orlando are both overwhelmed by love. Orlando is advised by a sympathetic courtier, Le Beau, to leave the court before the usurping Duke does worse than ignore him. He does, and — hinting at the wisdom of Orlando's departure — the usurping Duke exiles his niece Rosalind with no further explanation. Rosalind's cousin and friend Celia and the court jester Touchstone offer to accompany her to find Rosalind's father, the exiled Duke, in the Forest of Arden. Celia suggests that the women disguise themselves, and she chooses to become Aliena. Rosalind comes up with the idea of dressing as a young man and calling herself "Ganymede." Touchstone, as his name suggests, remains unchanged. Everybody is underway.

Act II

In Arden, the exiled Duke praises the new life away from court that he and his followers have found. It is physically harder, colder, and more demanding, but free from the flattery, hypocrisy, and deception of the society they have left. It is further lightened by the presence of Jaques, a melancholy retainer whose grumbling reflections on both court and forest the Duke loves to hear, although it isn't always clear whether Jaques is a satirist of the court's flaws or their best example.

Rosalind, Celia, and Touchstone arrive exhausted in Arden; Rosalind is delighted by it, Touchstone less so, Celia simply worn out. They meet Corin and Silvius, two of the forest's shepherds, and learn of Silvius's desperate love for a shepherdess, Phoebe. Corin invites them back to his cottage, regretting that he cannot do more for them. Celia decides "right suddenly" to buy the land and sheep Corin tends (2.4.99), and they all go to settle in.

As the Duke and his companions prepare a rustic feast, Orlando charges in and demands food at swordpoint to feed old Adam, who has collapsed from hunger and weariness. The Duke greets him hospitably, and tells him that he is welcome to share with them. Orlando is chastened, Adam is saved, and the exiled Duke welcomes them both to Arden.

Act III

Having learned of the flight of Celia, Touchstone, and Rosalind, and suspecting (wrongly) that they are with Orlando, the usurping Duke demands that Oliver reveal where Orlando is. When Oliver protests that he does not even like his brother, much less know where he is, the Duke commands him to deliver Orlando within the year. Oliver, too, finds himself bound for Arden, looking for Orlando.

Meanwhile, in the forest, Orlando is busy writing poetry to Rosalind and hanging it in the trees for anybody to read. Rosalind, Touchstone, and Celia — that is, Ganymede, Touchstone, and Aliena — wander in one by one, each with a small harvest of poems. Celia reveals that it is Orlando who has written the wooden rhymes; she discovered him lying under a tree and recognized him from the wrestling match. Rosalind is both thrilled and horrified.

Orlando and Jaques take a quick and cordial dislike to one another. Rosalind introduces herself to Orlando as Ganymede and begins to chat him up. Orlando explains that he is desperately in love with Rosalind. Ganymede doubts it — Orlando doesn't look nearly sick enough to be in love. But he offers to cure Orlando of it by letting him get the wooing out of his system on Ganymede, who will pretend to be Rosalind. Orlando does not think much of this kind of talking cure, but Ganymede reassures him and Orlando agrees to at least one session.

Touchstone scares up a love interest of his own, the shepherdess Audrey. Although his appreciation of her is as ambivalent as his feelings about the forest, he finds a priest to marry them anyway, the tellingly-named Oliver Martext. Corin shows Ganymede and Aliena to another struggling pair, the high-minded and infatuated Silvius, and Phoebe, who is not interested in him at all. But Phoebe likes what she sees in Ganymede very much, despite his attempts to brush her off, and after Ganymede and Aliena leave, Phoebe recruits Silvius to deliver Ganymede a letter from her.

Act IV

Orlando appears for his first love therapy session, late. Rosalind — in fact Rosalind as Ganymede as Rosalind — tries to lead Orlando through some basic lessons in love and gets as far as rehearsing a wedding ceremony before Orlando has to go dine with the exiled Duke. He promises to return. Silvius comes in with Phoebe's letter. Then Oliver unexpectedly appears with another, still less welcome message for Ganymede. Coming to Arden to seek out Orlando, Oliver had fallen asleep and was about to be attacked by both a poisonous snake and a lion. Luckily Orlando stumbled across him and chased off the menagerie, but was injured while protecting Oliver. Because of his wounds, Oliver explains, Orlando cannot make his next appointment. Orlando's display of fraternal love has completely altered Oliver, who feels himself a new man. Aliena thinks he is rather a nice one. Ganymede gets suspiciously woozy at the sight of Orlando's blood on the handkerchief.

Act V

Having settled on a priest, Touchstone and Audrey are limping for better or worse towards marriage, but now they run into other problems: Audrey may already be betrothed to another shepherd, William. With a flurry of big words and loose reasoning, Touchstone convinces him that Touchstone has the better claim to her (proximity, apparently) and William, flummoxed, departs.

Now wholly reconciled, Oliver confesses to Orlando that he has fallen in love with and courted Aliena, and that, since they have decided to marry and live together in the forest, he is giving the family estate to Orlando. Ganymede is as surprised as Orlando by this sudden example of successful matchmaking, but Oliver's announcement seems to change Orlando's mood.

He is done courting by proxy, he says; he "can no longer live by thinking" (5.2.54). Ganymede promises him a resolution at Oliver and Celia's wedding the next day, and similarly assures Silvius and Phoebe of happy endings to their respective desires for Phoebe and for Ganymede at the wedding. If Ganymede can produce Rosalind, Orlando will marry her; if Phoebe then refuses to marry Ganymede, she will marry Silvius. All agree to meet at the wedding and, if Ganymede can satisfy them all, be married tomorrow. Touchstone and Audrey will join them. It looks as if a lot of loose ends, and spare bodies, may be bound up at once.

At the wedding the next day, Ganymede and Aliena slip out and return, undisguised, as Rosalind and Celia, in the company of Hymen, the pagan god of marriage. Orlando is thrilled to find that his boy was his girl all along; Phoebe is startled, but goes along with her promise to marry Silvius since Ganymede is no longer available. When Orlando and Oliver's middle brother, who confusingly is named Jaques like the Duke's grouchy retainer, unexpectedly shows up to say that usurping Duke has decided to restore the dukedom to his elder brother and to withdraw to the forest of Arden to follow a life of contemplation, all seems resolved. As the forest court prepares to leave Arden, melancholy Jaques (and not the middle brother) decides to stay in Arden with the usurping Duke-turned-hermit. The newly restored Duke announces that the wedding rites for all will begin — and the play is over. Rosalind lingers onstage to present the epilogue, and, while delivering it, changes slowly from girl character to boy actor. And the boy leaves the stage.

2

What is the play about?

As You Like It doesn't have a conventional theme, as we might say the theme of *Macbeth* is ambition or the core of *Romeo and Juliet* is love. Instead, it repeatedly and variously poses a question: *What if the world were other than it is?* Other ways the world could be are conjured through the characters' use of what Touchstone near the end of the play calls the "virtue in 'if'" (5.4.101). *As You Like It* is a set of experiments in which its characters conditionally change an aspect of their world and see what comes of it: what if I were not a girl but a man? What if I were not a duke, but a figure like Robin Hood, and my realm were not the artificial hierarchies of a ducal court but something more natural and democratic, a woodland band of cooperating near-equals? What if I were a deer? "What would you say to me now an [that is, "if"] I were your very, very Rosalind?" (4.1.64–65). And then, most importantly, what follows? Over the course of *As You Like It*, characters and audiences find out together by theatrically playing with other possibilities, talking some through, putting others into action, and gauging the outcomes. They experiment with other ways the world could be because the worlds they find themselves in are *not* as they like them. Over the course of the play, they come closer to learning what they do like, and how their world can be more as they like it.

The titles of Shakespeare's tragedies and histories point to the central figure around whom they pivot: *Hamlet, Othello, Henry V, Richard III*. The titles of his comedies, in contrast, hardly point anywhere: *A Midsummer Night's Dream, A Comedy of Errors, Much Ado About Nothing, Twelfth Night*—and, of course, *As You Like It*. It's sometimes assumed that the titles Shakespeare chose for comedies are throwaways, confections that could apply to any of a number of plays. *Twelfth Night*, we assume, was called that because it was performed on the twelfth night after Christmas. *All's Well That Ends Well* could really be used for almost any of Shakespeare's comedies, and actually doesn't fit the play it is attached to particularly well.

But with *As You Like It* it is hard not to feel a stronger affinity between the title and the play. The problem the play poses is not a simple connecting of dots, where boy meets girl, loses girl, finds girl again. That's the play's plot in a nutshell (unless maybe it begins girl meets boy, girl loses boy...), but *As You Like It* does not take it for granted that it knows what we, or it, or its characters, *would* like. Although Rosalind and Orlando are immediately drawn to each other, I suspect that if they were married at the end of the first act, before long they wouldn't really like each other all that much. They require the play to bring their different expectations about love and each other into tune. At the play's end, Jaques remains in Arden in part because he does not yet know what he likes. The title *As You Like It* raises a question more than it makes a statement. What *is* as you like it? What is it that you really like or want? *As You Like It* doesn't tell us that it knows what we like and will give it to us. It asks us find out.

To ask "what if?" is a favorite tactic of Shakespeare's. What if someone were betrothed to both a man and a maid (Olivia in *Twelfth Night*)? What if two men loved the same woman—and then for some reason fell in love with her best friend (Lysander and Demetrius in *A Midsummer Night's Dream*)? What if a prince learned that his father had been murdered by his uncle for his crown and his queen? What if a Moor became an honored general in the Venetian army, but then married the daughter of a senator? It's not hard to frame most of Shakespeare's plays as enactments of this kind of thought experiment. But in most of his other plays, the characters are the experiment and the audience is — well, the audience, observing and appraising the outcomes of the plot.

In *As You Like It,* the characters themselves are both experiment and experimenters. They do what they can to find out what the world would be like if certain things in it were different than they are. They do not, that is, begin from scratch, but in a world that they find themselves in, a world that they must begin, at least, by accepting as given. The first step every experimenter in *As You Like It* makes is to imagine, deeply and immersively, some particular change in the world as it is, and then to explore speculatively and performatively what follows from that change: to act it out. With greater or lesser degrees of self-consciousness, these experiments all begin with a hypothesis, an "if". The characters assert something about the world that they know is not the case, and this fiction lets them act out what would happen if it were — and not only *if it were,* but something, not otherwise apparent, about *how it is now.* Rosalind, for instance, can become Ganymede, and then invite Orlando to let Ganymede become Rosalind. Together they work (or act) out answers. As Ganymede, Rosalind confirms her guess that young men have a different kind of liberty than young women, but also that they have some unexpected obligations (to behave in a "manly" way, whether that is not quailing at violence or not flirting with attractive men like Orlando) and some similar constraints (Ganymede seems to be as vulnerable to sexual predation as Rosalind, when Jaques approaches her). Practicing his courtship on Ganymede as if Ganymede were Rosalind (Orlando's hypothesis is unusually lucky), Orlando discovers that it is not enough to muse on his beloved and then to kiss her (or, alternately, die in his "own person" [4.1.85]). He must talk with her and listen to her as well.

There are many experimenters in *As You Like It,* and in their experiments they work over and under one another, interfere with one another, complement and divert one another. They produce not one other possible world but many, as many and more as the characters onstage. They are not as powerful as Shakespeare's later technicians of the possible, like Prospero in *The Tempest* or Paulina in *The Winter's Tale,* and they lack the magical abilities of *A Midsummer Night's Dream*'s confident, incompetent Oberon and Puck to change how others view the world. On the other hand, they are not as helplessly lucky as Viola, Orsino, and Olivia in *Twelfth Night,* who discover in Viola's twin brother Sebastian a painless doubling that redistributes an awkward threesome evenly into two couples; or as paralyzed as Hamlet, who seems baffled by the way things are not as he would have them be and in the end finds — perhaps — that the best he can do is take them as they are and let be.

The characters of *As You Like It* stand at a hinge of thought and action, conscious that they desire something, but not wholly capable of getting it. Their desires move them in ways they do not fully control, as Touchstone sees: "As the ox hath her bow, sir, the horse his curb, and the falcon her bells, so man hath his desire" (3.3.73–74). One's desire is like a burden, then, or a telltale, something that puts its bearer to service and sets him or her working in the world. Before they begin their experiments, it is not even clear what the play's characters like, and what you like, even (or especially) to them. This is how a nineteenth-century preoccupation with character gets so much right (I find myself beginning this essay with characters, for instance, and not themes) and is still so wrong. It takes for granted that the characters are complete and fixed, and that the play gradually reveals their complexity. But it is much more as if the characters start out relatively incomplete and uncomplicated, and then, by testing their desires against what the world gives them, put themselves in much more complicated, much less presumed, relations to both world and desire. Their awareness that the world could be different than it is, is a step towards making it something that they wish it to be, and towards learning what that is. This is most obvious in the characters the play focuses on, like Orlando, Rosalind, Touchstone, or Jaques. But the play gives us a sense that if we were to look more deeply and more widely, we would see that all the characters — Oliver, the exiled Duke, Corin, Audrey, Adam — are no less engaged in trying to imagine and to realize a world more as they like it. And not only the play's characters are experimenting to discover what they like. The stagings of the events that the characters of the play undertake, the play suggests, are also attempts to find something for its audiences, as they like it.

The psychoanalyst D.W. Winnicott distinguished two ways people can think about alternative realities: *fantasying,* which is omnipotent but also dissociates the thinker from a lived reality into a daydream, and *playing,* where anticipations, projections, and hypothetical actions are constantly exchanging with reality, transforming it and being transformed. For the most part, *As You Like It*'s experimenters *play* in the play, allowing what is real to press back against what they would like it to be (Silvius seems a notable exception, and when he says that to be a lover "is to be made all of *fantasy*" [5.2.90, my emphasis], he is using the word almost in Winnicott's sense: disconnected *fantasy* is precisely Silvius's Petrarchan problem). Their playing is what makes *As You Like It experimental* rather than *fantastic*: by thinking through or acting out these changes, characters get to see some of the consequences they bring with them, some of the resistances that foreclose them, and some of the opportunities they unexpectedly open. These consequences aren't always welcome, and they are rarely what their initiators expected: "what shall I do with my doublet and hose?" (3.2.212–13) asks Rosalind in frustration when it turns out that crossdressing is liberating in some ways and confining in others. That is the importance of putting imaginings into action, or at least into voice. It is what separates the play as *playing* from utopian dreaming or *fantasying,* where every story marvelously ends as its dreamer wills it.

We think of Shakespeare as working in and making *theater,* but the word he and his contemporaries used more often for what they did was *playing.* It's not a huge distinction, but there are differences in what each word expresses — each way of categorizing the shared activity of actors, the tiremen who outfitted them with costumes and props, their writers and bookkeepers, audiences, the gatherers who collected their pennies, and all the others whose labor first realized *As You Like It* and other plays in England in the 1590s.

The word *theater* comes from a Greek word that means *to look*; the same word is the origin of words like *theory*. *Theater* was not a common word, at least in English. Its Latin form *theatrum* was well known to every schoolboy who was trained in the writings of Terence, and what may have been the first purpose-built playhouse in London was given the proper name *The Theater* in 1576, but up until the middle of the sixteenth century, when it appears in English, it is almost always defined or translated, as "a common beholding place," for instance. Even when it came into more common use, *theater* retains something of its learned feel. It is — surprisingly, perhaps, to us — a little bookish. A faint etymological vibration from its Greek origins resonates in it, and the word suggests a kind of distanced vision, a spectacle held at arm's length and taken in through the eye or perhaps the ear, one that its audience beholds but in which it does not take part.

Playing, in contrast, is all in. It takes the whole body, both of its performers and of its watchers, and while these two groups have different roles, they are equally involved in the action that they make. Like players in any other kind of game, the people who come together at a stage play commit to its rules, and their shared participation makes it happen. *Play* became a subject of study for psychologists, sociologists, philosophers, and cultural critics in the twentieth century; their many different approaches agree on play's centrality to thinking and living and its startling combination of intense seriousness, deep absorption, and lack of necessity. Scholars as varied as Winnicott, educator Jean Piaget, and cultural historian Johan Huizinga all put play at the center of human activity, echoing the observation of Friedrich Schiller — an admirer and translator of Shakespeare — that the human is most fully human in the freedom of its play. This kind of creative, open-ended *play* is a much better description of what *As You Like It* is about than purely speculative *theater*.

Some figures, like Jaques, would rather step back and observe and critique, but they are no less at play than Rosalind with her multiple disguises or Touchstone and the clever schemes that always seem to swirl around him and sweep him up with them. And the audiences of *As You Like It* are also involved, if they allow themselves to be, plotting ahead with Rosalind or Orlando towards unforeseen outcomes.

By exploring ways the world can be different than it is, the characters of *As You Like It* strive to make the world a place in which they can be at home, not as a utopia — Arden may promise that, but certainly doesn't fulfill it — but as an ongoing work of living. More than any other Shakespearean comedy, *As You Like It* resists the closure of "happily ever after." Part of the play's brightness is that it shows living itself as an ongoing, difficult, unresolved, but ultimately *happy* task. Thus Touchstone woos Audrey, praises "the gods for thy foulness," and hopes that "sluttishness may come hereafter" (3.3.36–37); Oliver and Celia give up their social station to "live and die...shepherd[s]" in Arden (5.2.12); Phoebe acknowledges that Silvius's steady "faith" has won her "fancy" (a word which is after all only another way of saying *fantasy* [5.4.148]); Jaques and the usurping younger brother of the Duke stay in Arden to contemplate their worlds further, perhaps never to return (although who can imagine that Jaques, no less driven by the world than Touchstone, will not come back in some other guise, in some unwritten Act Six?). We get a sense at the play's end not that things have been settled once and for all, but that the characters have taken time to breathe — to live in their new situations until they discover better ones, or until they discover new desires.

3

What's in a name?

The pasts of the main figures in *As You Like It* are as unsettled as their futures at the play's end. Shakespeare regularly borrowed characters, settings, plot points, and whole stories from previous writers; so did most of his contemporaries, who did not think much of originality but deeply admired tradition, even when they were actively changing it. Like the play's title, the names of many of the characters are suggestive, all the more surprisingly so because, when read in other ways, they could seem to be so derivative. But the distances between some of the origins for these characters and their outcomes in Shakespeare's play are striking, and hint again that an important part of the play is imagining things otherwise.

The most direct source for the name of the play's heroine, Rosalind, is Thomas Lodge's prose romance of nearly a decade before, *Rosalynde* (1590), which also gave Shakespeare the bones of his plot. Its heroine Rosalynde is also the daughter of an exiled nobleman; also escapes to a forest of Arden disguised as a boy, Ganimede, to join her father; and also brings her inseparable friend, who in the romance is named Alinda and renames herself in disguise as Aliena, like Celia. Lodge's *Rosalynde* also features a younger son who runs away from a cruel older brother to the forest of Arden; an unhappy shepherd wooing an uninterested shepherdess; a clutch of plaintive sonnets; and most of the play's startling reversals and happy endings. Sound familiar yet? Shakespeare also gives the name Rosaline to a particularly sparky princess in *Love's Labors Lost,* and Rosalind is Romeo's first love, who never appears onstage. In *Antonio and Mellida,* a play produced about the same time as *As You Like It,* a Rosalind is a witty counselor-in-love to the heroine.

More intriguingly, a Rosalind appears in Edmund Spenser's *Shepheard's Calendar* (1579), a widely influential collection of a dozen pastoral poems keyed to the months of the year, with extensive and perhaps joking explanatory notes by a commentator "E.K.," who may be Spenser himself. In the first poem of the sequence, "Januarye," Rosalind is a shepherdess eagerly courted by Colin, a shepherd whom E.K. explains is a figure for the poet. (Is there any of Colin in *As You Like It*'s Corin, the kind shepherd who welcomes Rosalind and company to Arden?) Of "Rosalind" E.K. explains, "Rosalind is also a feigned name, which being wel ordered, wil bewray the very name of hys [that is, the writer of the *Calendar*'s] loue and mistresse, whom by that name he coloureth" — perhaps even one of Queen Elizabeth's pastoral avatars, as she was frequently imagined by courtier poets looking to ingratiate themselves with her. Still more interestingly for Shakespeare's play, Colin is being timidly courted with gifts by an older shepherd, Hobbinol, but he is not interested. Rather crassly, Colin hands them over to his own object of desire: "Ah foolish Hobbinol, thy gifts bene vayne: / Colin them gives to Rosalind againe" ("Januarye," 59) This prompts E.K. to anxiously weigh love between men and women against love between men and boys, and to prefer the latter, "pederastic" kind (written coyly by E.K. in Greek), while rejecting with vigor all kinds of "execrable and horrible sinnes of forbidden and unlawfull fleshlinesse." While Shakespeare's most immediate debt is to Lodge, something of Spenser's Rosalind has also seeped into Shakespeare's. Spenser's Rosalind suggests a rejection of same-sex desire (Colin chooses her over Hobbinol) at the same time that Shakespeare's Ganymede evokes it. E.K.'s endorsement of spiritual, "Platonic" same-sex love, and preference of it to heterosexual, physical love, complicates things further.

Disguised as Ganymede, Shakespeare's Rosalind adds another layer of complication to the already complicated formula of Elizabethan boy-acting by offering to play a girl — in fact, to play Rosalind — for Orlando to practice his wooing on. The name she chooses when she goes into exile, Ganymede, is suggestive, to say the very least. Ganymede was, famously, the cupbearer of the gods, but he became their cupbearer after Jupiter saw him and desired him so passionately that he swooped him up to Olympus. Ganymede appears in Ovid's *Metamorphoses* rather chastely, less so in the first scene of Christopher Marlowe's *Dido Queen of Carthage,* where he offers to "spend [his] time in [Jupiter's] bright arms" (1.1.22). The word *catamite,* slang for a boy prostitute or any male who was a sexual partner for other men, was supposedly derived from the name. But in other intellectual traditions from Plato onwards, Ganymede assumed a very different valence, representing the desire to exceed the physical world and rise to the divine. The name "Ganymede" thus came to Shakespeare with two significations in apparent conflict, as an emblem of the destructive passions of same-sex desire and as a representation of the human spirit borne aloft by its intellectual desire for the divine. Leonard Barkan beautifully characterizes this transvaluation as "[w]hat might be said to be the most illicitly carnal of all the divine amours is translated into the most positively sanctioned." Ganymede thus emblematizes both the loftiest of human aspirations, to soar aloft in contemplation, and what was then considered a degrading and unnatural imprisonment in the mire of earthly, physical pleasure.

It isn't clear from the play if Rosalind ever tells Orlando that she is (a) Ganymede. Perhaps by the time she discovers that Orlando is also in Arden and wishes she were no longer wearing her boy's clothes ("Alas the day, what shall I do with my doublet and hose?" [3.3.184–85]), she no longer finds this situation so funny. But Rosalind gives the highly wrought figure of Ganymede a comic turn, as the pleasures she offers are really those of clever conversation and companionship, and her wisdom is of a very worldly and practical kind: "[M]en have died from time to time and worms have eaten them, but not for love" (4.1.97–99). But it is not hard to see at the same time something of the desire for eternity in Ganymede that some of Shakespeare's contemporaries did.

So much for the figures of Rosalind and Ganymede, and the changes that Shakespeare discovers in them. The male protagonist in Lodge's *Rosalynde,* the source that Shakespeare imitated for the plot of *As You Like It,* is called Rosader. Where did "Orlando" come from? The foreign name was familiar to English readers of Shakespeare's time as the Italian version of the name "Roland" (which, interestingly, is the name of Orlando's father, Roland or Rowland de Boys, "Roland of the Woods" — perhaps in some sense cueing us to see that Orlando is his father's proper heir, and that Arden is where he will come into his inheritance). The bold knight Orlando's multifarious adventures, spread across many works and authors in an overlapping band of chivalric romances, make up a disaggregated Renaissance prequel to the events of the medieval *Chanson de Roland.* In these tales, Oliver is Orlando's closest friend; Shakespeare makes him Orlando's unfriendly older brother. The most famous of these romances were Boiardo's *Orlando Inamorato* ("Orlando in Love") and Ariosto's *Orlando Furioso* ("Orlando Enraged"), handily describing Orlando's two moods in *As You Like It. Orlando Furioso* was translated into English by John Harington in 1591, and the beginning of *Orlando Inamorato* was translated into English in 1598, not too long before Shakespeare's play was first performed. In Ariosto's often tongue-in-cheek version, Orlando goes mad with jealousy at being deserted by the woman he loves and rampages through the countryside, destroying everything in his path. Shakespeare's Orlando has something of the same violence in him. He beats Charles the wrestler brutally, and when Oliver calls him a villain, the text makes it clear that Orlando grabs him by the throat, releasing him with the scarcely reassuring words, "Wert thou not my brother I would not take this hand from thy throat till this other had pulled out thy tongue for saying so" (1.1.55–58). He tries to take food for Adam from the exiled Duke and his followers at swordpoint (2.7). The Duke gently suggests that Orlando will do better with kind words than violence, and while part of his education in *As You Like It* is in the ways of love, another part is in gentleness.

While Shakespeare could have read Harington's Ariosto (or perhaps even Ariosto's Italian), a more likely point of contact for his Orlando is Robert Greene's play *Orlando Furioso*, first performed probably in the mid-1590s. Greene narrows down Ariosto's sprawling tale of intercontinental love and war to the episode in which Orlando finds the name of his beloved carved into the trees of "Ardenia wood" (Arden also makes an early and insignificant appearance near the beginning of Ariosto's *Orlando Furioso*, where you might find it if you didn't read very far) and linked to another man (this turns out to be a cunning plot by Orlando's enemy Sacripant to drive him crazy). This much simpler framework gives Greene ample opportunities for Orlando to declaim wildly and to inventively pummel other actors. One group, for instance, is thumped with a leg that Orlando has just torn off a shepherd. Greene's Orlando is finally reconciled with his beloved after a set of gratuitous combats with his fellow knights. When Orlando in *As You Like It* threatens his brother, or throws Charles to the ground, audience members might have recalled Greene's earlier, more tempestuous Orlando. If so, Orlando's willingness to learn less angry ways might have come as a surprise to them.

4

What happens when Rosalind dresses as a boy?

Having lost their homes, their families, and their status (1.3), Celia and Rosalind respond by doubling down. They give up still more and try something new. Celia decides to "put myself in poor and mean attire / And with a kind of umber smirch my face" (1.3.101–2), and suggests Rosalind do the same. But Rosalind has another idea:

> Were it not better,
> Because I am more than common tall,
> That I did suit me all points like a man? (1.3.104–5)

It is the play's first, longest, and deepest experiment in imagining the world as other than it is. Rosalind notes how she is already like a man and deduces what she will need to be more like a man, in this case some decent props and costuming (it cannot be an accident that both Rosalind and the play repeatedly designates maleness by a male outfit, "doublet and hose," for instance at 2.4.6, 3.2.190–91, 3.2.212–13, and 4.1.162). Rosalind concludes by distinguishing what she can change and what she can't:

> [I]n my heart

> Lie there what hidden woman's fear there will.
> We'll have a swashing and a martial outside
> As many other mannish cowards have
> That do outface it with their outward semblances. (1.3.108–12)

The fuzzy logic of "mannish" expresses what it is that allows Rosalind to put this "what if...?" into effect. The word is ambivalent about whether or not it points to a *man*. It can characterize Rosalind in her disguise as well as the "other...cowards" she distinguishes herself from. They *are* men and she *is not* one, but both she and they are *like* men, close to the qualities that mark or make a man. For Rosalind to be mannish, like a man, is to be closer to being a man than she is; for the cowards, being only *like* a man is further from being the men they should be. "Mannish" and like words of likeness find space between *seeming* and *being,* which Rosalind and the "cowards" approach from different directions. Likeness and likening do two things at once: they confirm distances, between one thing and what it is like, and between the things and those who assert their likeness; and they reveal the hidden symmetries and resemblances that bring things closer together. As Robert Watson puts it, even the title *As You Like It* "places 'like' as a barrier between 'you' and 'it'". Bruce Smith sees the force of the claim made by the title differently: "'Like' implicates *you* in *it*". The "mannish cowards" are in Watson's camp; Rosalind is in Smith's.

Here, early in the play, Rosalind speaks of what *is* as lying inside what only *seems*: what *is* makes a kind of true core that can be dressed up but not, finally, denied. She uses forms of the word "out" three times in three lines: her "martial outside" will "outface" her fearful woman's heart just as cowards' "outward semblances" do theirs. She proposes to Celia that, disguised as a man, she will be just as successful at warding off danger as any other outward-seeming man. In other words, Rosalind explains *why* and *how* she disguises herself as a boy, whether or not we buy it. *As You Like It,* though, is less interested in Rosalind's decision than in its consequences, in *what happens* when Rosalind becomes a boy. The difference between causes and consequences is, in a sense, the play's preoccupation as it imagines alternatives to how things are. To shift from causes to consequences tilts the relation of *being* to *seeming* from that of *inner* and *outer* to that of *before* and *after*. Appearances can be stripped away, core truths uncovered. But it is hard to the point of impossibility to return to a past, and scarcely any easier — at least in *As You Like It* — to see the past as wholly, predictably contained in the present, or the present in the past. Rosalind has her reasons for disguising herself as Ganymede, but these are quickly outstripped by her changed reality as she begins to act and interact as him. In the love lesson Ganymede does not simply put on Rosalind again, and at the end of the play Rosalind cannot simply take off Ganymede. The Rosalind she becomes by becoming Ganymede is not the same one she was. One consequence of being Ganymede is that Rosalind needs to invent a history to explain to Orlando how a youth native to Arden exhibits such a refined and graceful accent, even though she is striving to sound like a "saucy lackey" (3.3.286–87; her father the exiled Duke may hear this as well when he asks Ganymede's parentage, 3.5.30). Another is that she attracts the unwanted amorous attentions of Phoebe (3.6) and perhaps of Jaques too, who asks to be "better acquainted" with the "pretty youth" (4.1.1–2). (It's also possible that Jaques is not fooled by the disguise and wants to be better acquainted because he sees that Ganymede is a woman, or that he's just lonely.) A new identity in Rosalind's present, in other words, demands a new past and projects a changed future. It quickly goes beyond simply concealing a present (and past, and future) truth. She is less in disguise than inhabiting a different history, bound for a different future.

But Rosalind's transformation into Ganymede has other consequences as well. It makes sense to see Rosalind as leading Orlando through their lessons in love when she takes back her role as Rosalind while still in the character of Ganymede. But Rosalind also changes in these exchanges, becoming more capable of realizing what she wants in love, and coming to see how she can get what she hopes for from her desire. Rosalind is immediately attracted to Orlando, but at their first meeting, as herself, Rosalind is scarcely able to speak to him ("Not a word?" asks the astonished Celia in the next scene [1.3.2]), far from the quick intelligence and easiness she shows with Celia (1.2). In the next scene, though, Rosalind has already begun to imagine the world as different, precociously casting Orlando as her "child's father" (1.3.11). Celia warns her that it is easier to stick to familiar ways: "[I]f we walk not in the trodden paths, our very petticoats will catch" burrs (1.3.14–15). But *As You Like It* suggests that Rosalind will be able to avoid the burrs only by leaving the trodden paths behind, as well as her petticoats. Out of her petticoats and in Arden, pretending to be Ganymede pretending to be Rosalind, Rosalind recovers her voice. Ganymede can banter with and refuse Orlando with equal conviction. He can express sexual desires, as when he tells Orlando that he is as native to Arden "as the cony that you see dwell where she is kindled" (3.3.285), a sentence that can mean the rabbit that lives where it was born ... or, punning on "cony" as *vagina* and "kindled" as *sexually aroused,* something like the vagina you're looking at stays where it gets hot. He can also utter more domestic ones when, as Rosalind, he asks Celia to officiate at a play marriage (4.1).

Ganymede as Rosalind can also give voice to the concerns that married love will not be perfect, and that not every day will bring bliss. This Rosalind criticizes the stereotypical wife,

> more jealous of thee than a Barbary cock-pigeon over his hen, more clamorous than a parrot against rain, more new-fangled than an ape, more giddy in my desires than a monkey, (4.1.139–43)

so sharply that Celia threatens that "[w]e must have your doublet and hose plucked up over your head, and show the world what the bird hath done to her own nest" (4.1.162–64). But Ganymede's comical misogyny reflects Rosalind's concern for the sorry proposition that "men are April when they woo, December when they wed" (4.1.117–18) as much as Orlando's concern for the dangerous wife. When Hymen seals their match with the pledge that "[y]ou and you no cross shall part" (5.4.115), we are surer of Rosalind and Orlando because they have already uttered and enacted some of their crosses. The couple that marries at the end of the play are much changed from the pair who meet at the beginning, in ways that their earlier selves could not have guessed, or become, without their mutual dalliance with Ganymede.

When Rosalind offers Orlando her chain as a favor, she speaks of herself as "one out of suits with Fortune" (1.2.198), in the third person, as if she were not able to describe herself except as someone else. Rosalind can only be the self she really wants to be — the Rosalind who can love Orlando deeply and richly, as his equal, and be loved by him in the same way, not as the crystalline superlative that Orlando writes in his poems ("No jewel is like to Rosalind" [3.3.66]) but as a living person with hopes of her own — by pretending to be pretending to be that person.

Yes, two pretenses — one to be Ganymede and one to be Rosalind, again. It is something different to pretend to be yourself from the point of view of another. We could even say that Rosalind does not really know the self she wants to be until she experiences herself as something else, as the pretty, saucy Ganymede. Clothes do not simply make the man, as Jean Howard carefully shows in her discussion of the layers of Rosalind's disguises and roles. But neither is being a man, or a woman, as straightforward or stable a condition as Rosalind seems to think when she first plans her disguise. Acting like a man lets Rosalind change the way she understands the world — her desires, sexual, social, familial, friendly; her fears of what she may do and how those she loves may respond; her ambitions; above all, how she navigates and lives all of them.

5

Where is Arden?

"Well, this is the Forest of Arden" (2.4.12), declares Rosalind. What "this"? Although many nineteenth- and twentieth-century productions of *As You Like It* delighted in detailed sets of Shakespeare's transformative forest, in an Elizabethan production, on a relatively bare stage, Rosalind would have called Arden into being by saying those words. Rosalind's announcement is the play's watershed, a kind of shorthand demonstration of the role Arden plays in it. "The Forest of Arden," observes Juliet Dusinberre, a recent editor of *As You Like It,* "like Hamlet, like Falstaff, like Romeo and Juliet, has become a Shakespearean myth." As a myth, Dusinberre continues, Arden gestures in more than one direction. It contains not just variety, but contradiction, so that "in the Forest the polarity of real and ideal ceases to be illuminating." Even at its most material level, Shakespeare's Arden is at different times a pastoral oasis, a wintry wood, an impoverished waste. Part of Arden's fascination lies in its indeterminacy, and its indeterminacy begins in its name. Thomas Lodge's romance *Rosalynde* takes place in the wooded Ardennes, in France. *As You Like It* initially seems to follows suit with a whiff of French ornament: the Duke has a sympathetic courtier named Le Beau, Oliver and Orlando have first names are associated with the chivalrous heroes of French romance and are members of the de Boys family (French for "of the woods"). Dusinberre argues that the French Ardennes had gained some notoriety among English speakers as the site of a series of campaigns in the 1580s conducted by Robert Dudley, Earl of Leicester, one of Elizabeth's favorites, and Sir Philip Sidney, writer of the pastoral romance *Arcadia*. But there was another Arden closer to Shakespeare's home, the great forest of Warwickshire near Stratford. Arden was also the name of Shakespeare's mother's family. And of course Arden is also the Green World, a pastoral *locus amoenus,* an outlaw hideout akin to Robin Hood's Sherwood, and more mundanely a place where shepherds live and tend their sheep.

The many associations in the name "Arden," from geographical to personal, are part of what allows *As You Like It*'s forest to have the transformative part it plays. Arden occupies a pivot point in the first half of the play — Act 1 is taken up with getting the characters of the play into the forest, and Act 2 with recording their responses when they get there. Nobody enters it unchanged, it seems, from Rosalind's Ganymede to Oliver's or the usurping Duke's startling changes of heart. Unlike the nameless, moonlit wood of *A Midsummer Night's Dream,* Arden seems almost a character in its own right. Perhaps it would be better to call it a state of mind that different characters can fall into. With its unplaceable geography, Arden is first of all a place where what is presumed to be given by "reality" — the world as it is — is challenged by alternatives — worlds that might be. "The 'If' that Shakespeare ventures in *As You Like It,*" one critic notes, "is the Forest of Arden itself." For the play, it is *as if* we were transported to Arden. In the fiction of the play, to be in Arden is to be able to act *as if*: as if Rosalind were Ganymede or Arden were Eden, free from the "penalty of Adam" (2.1.5), first *as ifs* among many others.

In his aptly titled *Philosophy of As-If* (1911), Hans Vaihinger sketched some of the ways that people negotiate the thickets of reality by using fictions that simplify them, give them value, and otherwise organize them. Developing some of Vaihinger's theories, Frank Kermode observed that the mode of "as-if" — like, not accidentally, literary, dramatic, and poetic fictions — does not lend itself to proof or disproof. Instead, acting or behaving "as-if" is sustained and extended by the efforts of an author, actor, audience, or other imaginer. It can be maintained indefinitely, but lapses if its consistency is not attended to. Arden is what we might describe as an "as-if" space, where the given world is constantly subject to its alternatives, which can supplement but not replace the given world.

The Renaissance had several ways of imagining "as-if" realms like Arden. In *Shakespeare's Festive Comedy,* C.L. Barber detects what he called the "saturnalian pattern" of inversion in Elizabethan culture, including the core of Shakespeare's comic plays, a holiday regime of misrule that momentarily turned the order of the everyday upside down, mocked what had been serious and elevated what had been mocked. An exiled Duke of France might become "like the old Robin Hood of England" (himself a figure of festive inversion in Elizabethan England), his daughter the "pretty youth" Ganymede, and her fool an erstwhile courtier, as "the energy normally occupied in maintaining inhibition is freed for celebration." Taking his cue from Celia's exhortation "Now go we ... / To liberty and not banishment" (1.3.134–35), Barber sees the festive "release" of holiday as leading to "*clarification* ... a heightened awareness of the relation between man and 'nature' — the nature celebrated on holiday."

For Barber, though, "[T]he release of that one day was understood to be temporary license, a 'misrule' that implied rule," since "the natural in man is only one part in him, the part that will fade." Celebrating a rare "liberty" reconciled Elizabethans to the more lasting, less egalitarian and delightful demands of order and eternity that "translat[ed] ... liberty to bondage" (5.1.53–54). The ecstatic self-realizations of "release" were temporary, but the "*clarification*," as Barber understood it, was permanent, and rendered them back to their divisive stratifications. Barber's powerful reading, laid out largely in the language of *As You Like It,* helps place Arden, the theatrical institutions that represented it, and the culture that subsumed both of them, in its particular historical context. It was also germinal in New Historical approaches to the ways in which supposedly "subversive" moments — those that challenged the rules of gender-identification, or political or familial order, or erotic desire — might be "contained" by dominant cultural forces, in a lethal two-step that permits attempts to see the world otherwise only to recapture them.

To be sure, Arden can be seen as subversion contained — and perhaps in part must be, since the play undeniably ends in a restoration of most of the rules it began by challenging. Only most of them, though; and it is less clear, I think, that it *also* implies that its alternatives can be reduced to standing the rules on their heads. The literary critic Northrop Frye proposed that escapes like that to Arden were an innovation in the history of the genre of comedy. Before this Elizabethan turn, Frye claimed, comedies followed one of two models, both derived ultimately from classical comedy, either the topical, ebullient, and sometimes biting "Old Comedy" of Aristophanes, or the more staid, marriage-minded "New Comedy" of Menander, Plautus, and Terence. (Old and New Comedy got these names well after either kind was being produced, at least in Greece, so while Aristophanes did precede Menander, Frye treats them less as developmental stages than as simultaneous types.) Comedies in the vein of "Old Comedy" attacked the ways things were, exaggerating and mocking the status quo in the hopes of correcting it, or presenting fantastic utopian visions that simply ran away from it, sometimes both. Instead of taking the world on directly, "New Comedy" accommodated it, finding ways creatively and joyfully to resolve competing demands of everyday life, as for instance in the happy and unexpected couplings that end so many Elizabethan comedies. Incidentally, Barber finds Shakespearean comedy to be Aristophanic (that is, Old Comedy), in contrast to the "Terentian and Plautine" New Comedy models of most of his contemporaries.

The innovation of some Elizabethan plays, according to Frye, is in the presence of a second world alongside the characters' own — a world, for instance, like Arden. Both Old and New Comedy, Frye argued, take place in a single world, at best offering an unrealizable alternative to the world we live in. Rather than immediately tackling whatever problems face their heroes, either through the direct assault of satire, the fantastic escapism of utopian fictions, or some more plausible social reorganization like marriage and forgiveness, these Elizabethan plays release their comic heroes into a different, kinder landscape that shadows but softens the world they come from. Withdrawing to this friendlier second world, the characters find what they need to be renewed. Because this sheltering second world is imagined as innocent, natural, and harmonious, and because it is so often figured as a forest or garden, Frye, thinking of Shakespeare's Arden or his dreaming woods outside Athens, called it the Green World.

Green World comedies like *As You Like It* combine something of the impossible escapism of Old Comedy with the impossible attunement of conflicting impulses of the New. They differ from these forms because their characters pass from one world to another, from a world in which they cannot live fully to one in which they can heal, and then back again into a world that they newly find they have the power to transform. In the Green World, the protagonists rediscover something in themselves that had been lost or damaged in the real world. Renewed and refreshed, they return to revitalize the familiar world — a world Frye calls the "red and white," with its histories and conflicts — that they had left behind. The second world is a place of respite rather than escape; the world we live in is shown to be flawed but salvageable. Its problems still remain, only now the characters may be better prepared to face them, perhaps because they have learned something, perhaps because they have recovered something, perhaps something of both. And they must return: the Green World is an escape but not a place to live, sometimes a greater home but not the world in which humans must dwell and struggle.

Frye's schema of the Green World is particularly useful in thinking about what goes on in *As You Like It*. Almost all the principal characters flee to the forest of Arden, and almost all do so to get away from troubles at home, whether in the form of hostile brothers (Orlando), political exile (Rosalind), or both (the exiled Duke). Another group goes, though, for love or loyalty towards those who are fleeing the red and white of their worlds — Celia, Touchstone, Jaques and the other supporters of the exiled Duke. A few figures pursue their enemies into Arden seeking to destroy them, like Oliver and the usurping Duke. In the end, though, all register the impact of the new world that they enter when they enter Arden. Some, like Oliver, seem completely and instantly transformed by it. In others, the change is more subtle, like Orlando's from being regularly overcome by the violence of his emotions, sometimes even to the point of physical violence, toward greater self-control and greater awareness of himself and those around him. Others still seem scarcely to change course at all; Rosalind, for instance, seems only to become more fully herself. Most importantly, almost all figures return from Arden's Green World.

Predictably, Shakespeare's use of the trope of the Green World is more complex and contradictory than Frye's schematization of it. The usurping Duke and Jaques determine to stay in Arden to continue their contemplations. Their change of life is a continuing rejection of, or flight from, the world of white and red, at least for a time. When Oliver and Celia remain in Arden, however, we may see them as bringing something of the world of red and white into the Green, opening an ongoing narrative of family, sociability, and permanence within what had been the retreat in which Oliver was reformed and they found one another. And of course for the shepherds who already dwelt in Arden, the Green World was already scored by the inequities of the red and white. Corin, for instance, has the unpastoral problem of being a tenant of a landlord who does not support him.

Another literary critic, Harry Berger, revises Frye's notion of the Green World. Berger's Green World is not a naturally-given paradise, but a fiction of human making, into which we step out of the world to recover from it and to renew our sense of what is possible and good. It is, in other words, a fantasy, and it is the possibility of imagining how things could be different that restores its characters, not a real haven. As Berger notes, though, there is a danger that the seductive Green World may not supplement the real one, but annihilate it, so that its devisers become lost in a fantasy that is comforting but unreal. The world we hope for and imagine can come to seem as if it had been made *for* rather than *by* us, and we may not care to recover the richer, more abrasive, less tractable world of actual experience. We can trust in our fictions so fully that we come to believe in them and they become lies. Green World comedies reveal both our desire for something different and better, and the risks in consoling ourselves with it as if it could be an alternative to our world.

More recently still, Steve Mentz has suggested another angle on the Green World, namely the Blue World, so called for the sea as a place of intensity and change, pitched against Frye's restful Green World. The dangerous Blue World, as Mentz describes it, is something like a balancing opposite to Berger's dangerous Green one. Berger's Green World is the risk of giving oneself to one's fantasies, as if they could simply stand in for the world we are given. (Arden, at least, seems to insist that however our fantasies take hold of the world, and the world of our fantasies, the exchange is no simple one.) But the Blue World is radically careless of the human needs that literally traverse it, more than a passage between places, but never a destination. Although *As You Like It* is a thoroughly landlocked play (at least as much as Bohemia, which didn't stop Shakespeare from giving it a coastline), Mentz's sense of the uncaring sea as a fluid, mobile realm of transit hits Arden's mark, too. Arden may also be part of the Blue World, not a destination but a place of transformation and experiment which nevertheless never gives itself up entirely to those who play in it.

Shakespeare's Arden partakes of Barber's festive world, Frye's optimistic Green World, Berger's more doubtful one, Mentz's soundless Blue World, and D.W. Winnicott's distinction between play (which engages deeply, if indirectly, with reality) and fantasy (which tries to evade reality), as well as bringing something all its own. For *As You Like It* is full of fictions that its characters make up, and in which they believe with varying degrees of intensity and self-consciousness. It might be better to think instead of the Green *Worlds* of Arden, for Arden is no simple refuge from the difficulties of the worlds of the court or the family. It is closest to being a place of retreat and recovery for the exiled Duke, or for Rosalind and Orlando. But when the exiled Duke proclaims that the woods can teach him a moral lesson ("This our life.../ Finds tongues in trees, books in running brooks, / Sermons in stones, and good in everything" [2.1.15–17]), he comes very close to what Berger warns against, mistaking the experiment of the Green World for a new reality that has been given to him and that tells him what he wants to hear. Paradoxically, Orlando comes close to it, too, when he announces to Ganymede that he wants to end their practice courtship, because "I can no longer live by thinking" (5.2.49). While the Duke believes that the Green World of Arden is a kind of message to live in, Orlando turns away from it as if there were some solid reality that did not demand thinking to live in it. Neither sees that the power in Arden lies in its ability to offer alternatives to how things simply seem to be. To explore the extent and the limits of that power is left to figures like Rosalind, who tries to learn what she can do as a boy for herself as a woman; like Jaques, who tries to see the world as a deer might, and otherwise tries to imagine what his life might look like from outside it; or like Touchstone, who again and again explores the great virtue of "if."

6

Why do we hear about what Jaques said to a deer?

A favorite scene of nineteenth-century painters in *As You Like It* was Jaques sitting by the side of a stream, "weeping and commenting / Upon the sobbing deer" (2.3.65–66). This is not, of course, really a scene from the play, but something one of the exiled Duke's companions describes for the Duke: how Jaques describes the plight of the wounded deer to himself, or perhaps to the deer. Nobody in any of these exchanges, in other words, is speaking for themselves; everyone who speaks at all is trying to speak about the experience of another. Without seeing that they were doing it, Romantic painters of the melancholy philosopher moralizing upon a wounded stag were adding another layer of experience to those of the play, letting their own imaginings stand in for what they sought to picture, just like the Duke's man or like Jaques himself. How far it is possible to step into another's experiences, and how far we can remember that we are imagining and not experiencing them, is central to the question *As You Like It* repeatedly poses, *What if the world were other than it is?*

This overlaying of one experience upon another and relaying from one source to another is first of all what this scene calls attention to. The stag weeps but cannot speak. Jaques can give words to its pain, although they may not be the right ones. Stag and Jaques alike are set apart from the Lord who speaks of them and regards Jaques with, at best, a sense of bemusement. With each new layer between the wounded stag and its interpreters, we understand — even if none of the interlocutors handing on their own experiences of another's experience seem to — that the feelings being narrated can shift in tone. To the Lord who describes it and to the exiled Duke who begs to hear more, Jaques's behavior is edifying but not sympathetic: the Duke enthuses, "I love to cope him in these sullen fits, / for then he's full of matter" (2.1.67–68). To them Jaques is "moralizing" the events around the stag "into a thousand similes" (2.1.44–45). In other words, they see Jaques as seeking morals or lessons in what is happening to the deer, as if it were a kind of living Aesop's fable, by comparing it to similar things in human life. They rightly see this as revealing as much or more about Jaques as about the deer. Moralizing, Jaques offers them another moral example of how not to moralize (of course, the Duke and the Lord are moralizing, too).

This is at least partly right. But what the Duke criticizes in Jaques as moralizing is, from another perspective, simply the ability to lend words to things. Jaques is trying to put into words what the world is like for the deer. The Lord and the Duke look to the example of the stag (as voiced by Jaques) as the Duke looked at the winds of Arden, to tell them something about the human world (it is easy to see the moralizing of others, harder to see one's own). But Jaques is reaching for almost the inverse — he tries to grasp something of the deer's world, through the lens of a human-like "testament / As worldlings do" (2.1.47–48) of wished-for community, friendship, and civil bonds. The touchstone for Jaques's feeling for the stag is that, as Jaques imagines the experiences of the deer, he does not just describe or analyze. He feels for them, too. As he speaks, rightly or errantly, about the "sobbing" deer, Jaques also is "weeping" (2.1.65–66). Whatever his words do, however wide they may go of the mark, his feelings and actions draw him closer to those of the deer, and his own feelings seem inseparable from the effort to put the stag's feelings into words. When later the Duke says of Jaques, "I think he be transformed into a beast, / For I can nowhere find him like a man" (2.7.1–2), he may be more right than he knows.

Jaques's fellow-feeling, to be sure, has some pronounced limits. Robert Watson notes that Jaques's position leaning over the stream is the same as that of Narcissus, hinting perhaps at Jaques's self-absorption (though this is also the same as the position of the stag). Jaques seems to have no impulse at all to help the stag, and if he does gain some momentary insight into the reality of the stag's suffering, it does not seem to change how he behaves for long. He is cheerfully ready to eat the forest banquet (of the same deer?) before Orlando bursts in on the company (2.7) and he enthusiastically celebrates other hunts (2.5, 4.2). Jaques's empathy never moves him to action. He can imagine another world — a stag's — and even to some extent enter it, but he does not seem to be able to change the world he is in and which seems so tedious and distasteful to him. In his most striking speeches we can discern the difference between simply trying to picture other ways the world can be and actually trying to inhabit them, however fleetingly or imperfectly, as Rosalind does when she puts on the identity of Ganymede to see what her world will become.

The philosopher Thomas Nagel famously asked, "What Is It Like To Be a Bat?" and concluded, more or less, nothing. First, being a bat is its own thing. It isn't reducible to a set of qualities or discrete phenomena, much less any subset of them. Second, the problem of being *like* something, bat or not, doesn't seem to be one that bats pose themselves. If it is, we don't have evidence of it. Thus even a bat might not know or feel or *care* what it is like to be a bat; to grasp after that likeness (perhaps in something like one of Jaques's "similes") might itself be not to be like a bat. Merely asking the question may root us in our un-bat-likeness, or even sink us further into it.

Nagel's claim has uncharitably been called an argument from lack of imagination. But much depends on what you want to mean by *like,* as Rosalind as Ganymede discovered when the same cheek that can be "mannish" for her becomes Ganymede's girlish "constant red and mingled damask" (3.5.124). On the one hand, Nagel is convincing when he says that there really is nothing that is entirely like what it is to be a bat. In another way, though, there are a lot of things that being a bat is like, and a lot of things — not necessarily the same things — that it is like to be a bat. Being a bird is like being a bat. So is being a lemur. So is being a sonarscope. And so, finally, is being a person, in some ways. Nagel's article is a valuable caution against careless gestures of empathy. The problem with most of these is that when they ask, "What Is It Like to Be a Bat?", the question they answer is "What Is It Like For a Bat to Be Like Me?", as the Duke does when he asks about the wood's "native burghers," (2.1.23) by which he means the deer, imagined as citizens displaced by his reign. Jaques does it, too; the apartness that he recognizes in the abandoned deer is first of all his own. This can be a narcissistic kind of anthropomorphism, projecting oneself into what one is looking at, seeing oneself and taking it to be something else. But, as Jane Bennett points out, a "strategic anthropomorphism" can serve to move us even if it is not exact; it lets us tentatively feel a way towards what it is like to be a bat, or a deer, if not to know it or declare it definitively. The power of such anthropomorphism, Bennett suggests, may be not in getting things right, but in seeing how different they could be than they are.

In this case, the best cue to follow may not be any of the "similes" Jaques asserts, but the tears that he shares with the stag. In some ways the spoken "similes" are the least successful part of Jaques's imagining of the stag's world, because they say more about Jaques's sense of his own apartness from his community than anything about the stag. Since the Duke has just been speaking so fulsomely of the refreshing honesty of "our life" (2.1.15) in the forest, Jaques's words are an honest reminder of that life's inequities. Even the Duke recognizes that there is some kind of injustice in the hunting that sustains them, but Jaques speaks (or we are told he speaks) as if from the point of view of the deer, neither seeing them as the Duke's "poor dappled fools" (2.1.22), which patronizingly places him above them, nor as "native burghers," which puts them in a sylvan republic like the community the Duke's companions imagine for themselves (or perhaps again below it, as citizens to aristocrats). For Jaques, the wounded stag is not in a community: hunted within its own home, "[l]eft and abandoned of his velvet friend" (2.1.50), ignored by the "careless herd" that races past (2.1.52), the stag has been painfully singled out by its misfortune. Even the tears it drops into the stream Jaques sees as a kind of misguided attempt to reach beyond itself, but the stag's "testament" only adds more water to what already has enough (2.1.47–49), and finds no fellowship in adding more to more. Its only fellowship in the scene, in fact, seems to be with Jaques, who contagiously catches its grief.

This scene is Jaques's introduction. The audience hears about him before it sees him, and what it hears about is how he speaks. This is appropriate for Jaques, who seems to pass through *As You Like It* almost untouched by it. In the play he is almost purely a vocalized commentary, oddly detached from the interactions of the plot and standing to one side of the relationships that the other characters weave among one another. Unsurprisingly, he chooses to remain in Arden when most of the others leave: if he does not really belong in Arden, neither does he seem to be at home at court. But his disengagement also makes him one of the most important of the play's characters, and one of the most memorable. With Touchstone and Rosalind, Jaques is one of the three figures who are most adept at imagining the world otherwise. But if he seems less able to realize them, the worlds Jaques can see nevertheless range more widely from his own experience than any others in *As You Like It*. What Jaques would like is far from clear, even to Jaques. But at the end of the play, when he chooses to remain in Arden, it is easy to imagine Jaques studying not only to imagine worlds he likes better, but also how to bring them to life.

7

What does Jaques telling us about Touchstone telling time tell us about them?

Not long after hearing the report about Jaques's curious moralizing on, or empathizing with, the deer, we hear another report from Jaques himself, this one on hearing a "motley fool thus moral on [and certainly not empathize with, although he wags along with] the time" (2.7.29). This is, presumably, Touchstone, whom we've already encountered. These secondhand descriptions of the characters of Jaques and Touchstone, uttered within the drama by other characters with angles and interests of their own, are strangely static and strangely revelatory, almost like introductions in the list of *dramatis personae,* or like film stills that render some implication of narrative or relationship by freezing it in place. It is clear that Jaques identifies with the motley fool he sees, perhaps in the same way he identifies with the deer, and with similar limitations. But where the deer apparently gives Jaques an opportunity for moralizing on his own, the fool can apparently see, or say, something that Jaques cannot apprehend without him. In response Jaques neither speaks nor weeps, but laughs; he returns to the Duke to ask the favor of putting on motley himself, so he can take the role of the fool on his own (perhaps he, or the play, is looking ahead to his speech later in the scene on the many parts a man plays in his time?).

The fact that Jaques here takes on the task of moralizing the moralizing of Touchstone pulls these two figures together within the play's worlds. Touchstone and Jaques are linked as the two most pronounced outsiders in Arden and the most outspoken critics of everyone else in the play. Their roles otherwise, though, are very different. Even in the accounts of the weeping deer and the clock in the forest, Jaques's effort to moralize the deer contrasts sharply to Touchstone's ataraxia, merely observing the passing of the time and noting "thereby hangs a tale" (2.7.28) without offering even to say what it is. Jaques's tears are one kind of empathy, and so is his laughter at Touchstone, but they seem as careful as his moralizing; Touchstone's letting-be, his acknowledgement that he, too, wags with the time, ripening or rotting, whether he will or not, is a very different sort. Touchstone, merry, earthy, hot after Audrey like "the horse his curb" (3.3.73–74), is quick with a quip to pick out the errors of others. He is a partner in fooling, and shines in the back and forth of conversation, where his questions and sharp observations nearly socratically lure those he talks to into the absurdities of their shared world. Jaques, in contrast, is a soloist: sullen, pensive, given to elaborately set speeches and imaginings, more often the butt of laughter than its instigator, and seeking above all to amuse himself. He is also the Rorschach test of the play. One nineteenth-century critic observed, "[H]e came to life again a century later as an English clergyman; we need stand in no doubt as to his character, for we all know him under his later name of Lawrence Sterne," the author of *Tristram Shandy*; in 1856 the French intellectual George Sand made him the central character in her adaptation of the play, and he is, depending on who you want to listen to, "the first light and brilliant pencil-sketch for Hamlet," "Hamlet *avant la lettre*," or "so much removed ... from Hamlet."

But in this play of liking, what do Touchstone and Jaques like? Both are quibblers and wordsmiths, although Jaques works harder at edifying and Touchstone at deconstruction.

Touchstone seems to have almost no interest in the "as if" questions posed by the other characters, although (or because) he is the character who most clearly indicates their parameters. For him, they seem a thoroughly disenchanted instrument: they either work as he wishes (as when he chases William off with his doubletalk) or not (as when Corin's resolute literalmindedness seems to stump even Touchstone). If anything, Touchstone prefers a playfully Ovidian uncoupling of words and worlds in which language generates its own internal conundrums and touches the world not at all. When he says to Audrey, "I am here with thee and thy goats, as the most capricious poet, honest Ovid, was among the Goths" (3.3.5–7), his words intricately call attention to themselves. *Goats* and *Goths* are near homophones, and *capricious* (from Latin *caper*, or goat) links the poet Ovid to both even as the sentence asserts his difference. But it has almost nothing to say about anything in the world, beginning with the fact that Ovid was notoriously not "honest" in any sense — any more than Touchstone is like him. Jaques, in contrast, seems to have been almost taken over by the as-if games he plays. There does not seem to be much in his life beyond his as-if thought experiments, and he tends to forget that they are, in fact, *experiments*.

The names of Touchstone and Jaques serve as an index to the difference of what they do in the play. A *touchstone* was a kind of dark stone that was used in the sixteenth and seventeenth centuries to test the purity of gold or silver alloys. Drawing the metal across the stone left a streak, the color of which varied depending on the precious metal content. It indicates, in other words, the value of something else, without having any value of its own. *Jaques* is of course a variant of *Jacques*; as Jacques it fits the intermittently French setting of Arden, and it is also the name of Oliver and Orlando's middle brother (and it is astonishing, if logistically daunting, to imagine that somehow he might be such a brother, unrecognized). But a *jaques* or *jakes* — both spellings appear — is also a common Elizabethan word for a privy. This is another humble device with an important function. It receives the filth that people produce as they go about their lives and removes it out of their way.

Touchstone, like Feste in *Twelfth Night,* is a "corrupter of words" and a cartographer of the possible, investigating what can be through the great virtue of "if," the word that posits a condition and simultaneously denies its reality. To invert the terms of Feste's and Touchstone's office, Jaques is more of a conserver of notions than a corrupter of words; he costively preserves and holds onto matter and then reveals it in unexpected depth and intensity. Like Touchstone, he can peel back the pretensions and assumptions of those around him, but he tends to replace them with assumptions of his own, generally more bitter but no more complete. He is so assured of the profundity of what he says that it becomes for him simply and obviously right. Jaques knows no "if", only "is." This makes him a kind of fundamentalist of thinking: he can imagine other worlds, but he does not know he is making them up, and above all he cannot imagine that what he imagines might be wrong. He can "suck melancholy out of a song as a weasel sucks eggs" (2.5.10–11), but never notices that this means that every song will be the same to him.

Like his namesake, Touchstone measures the value of other's words and deeds. Sometimes his test shows them to be wanting; sometimes, perhaps, they pass. He does not produce anything of value; he gauges the value of what others do. Jaques, like his namesake, is literally full of shit — unpleasant and unproductive. It may thus be harder to appreciate Jaques than Touchstone. It looks a little as if whatever Jaques touches turns to trash or as if all he does is paddle in excrement. But these are not only his own excrements, and perhaps he protects the others who also produce them from their most noxious effects.

8

What is pastoral?

When he leads his cast one by one to the forest of Arden, Shakespeare drops them into a long and well-developed tradition in European literature called *pastoral*. Pastoral writing represents an idealized form of rural life, nostalgically imagined as simpler, purer, and more honest, and offers it as a form of critique of life in centers of power like the city or the court. The name comes from the Latin word for shepherd, *pastor*, because shepherds and their country companions, like fauns, nymphs, or milkmaids, are its most frequent protagonists. By and large, the shepherds of pastoral live in a golden world, or at least a gilded one — they work, but not too hard; they enjoy the refreshment of simple, delicious foods, like honey or wine, and wholesome entertainments like song contests. They are for the most part hale and whole in their humble station. To be sure, their world is not without griefs. By and large, though, they are represented as being free from serious cares — cares their audience would take as serious, anyway. They may suffer unrequited love, be bested in a singing contest, argue over whose rams are finer, be forced from their lands by conflicts in the wider world, or even lose a beloved friend to death. But their lives are honest and fulfilling and unalloyed. Sadness and joy alike are deeply, richly, and uncomplicatedly felt, passionately, fully, and unfeignedly expressed, and lovely. As this synopsis suggests, pastorals and the emotions they explore are viewed from a nostalgic perspective that is quite different from their own. Their happiness and sadness are lovely because pastorals were made and enjoyed by the people who were most different from what they portrayed and of whose lives pastorals are most critical: the sadder but wiser elites of the cities and courts.

To modern readers, the lives of shepherds may seem at best marginally interesting, but pastoral must have had a great appeal, even if it is hard for us to feel it ourselves. Renaissance literary theory assigned to pastoral a prominence like that of comedy or tragedy. But it is very hard to define what pastoral is, beyond Paul Alpers's lucidly literal-minded insistence that it is what concerns the lives of shepherds. For one thing, it comes in an extraordinary range of forms. There are pastoral plays, both tragic and comic, pastoral poems, and pastoral episodes also occur in longer forms like novels and romances. Pastoral may represent the city through the country, nature from the point of view of art, or their simple opposition; it may depict an ideal of the leisured life or a pathetic fallacy in which the world reflects the emotions of a poem's protagonists; it may serve to introduce what William Empson in *Seven Types of Ambiguity* identified as a double perspective characteristic of the mode, a "clash between different modes of feeling," simultaneously innocent and experienced. What all of these possibilities share is a commitment to thinking about a familiar world of experience by representing a world that it is not. As Wolfgang Iser puts it, in pastoral "the real world is abstract and the unreal concrete." Pastoral art was a way for people who were *not* shepherds, from classical antiquity through to the Renaissance, to imagine concretely an easier, more forgiving world than the one they inhabited.

In its exploration of another world, we can see the affinity of pastoral to *As You Like It*'s more far-ranging interest in imagining how else the world might be. But in *As You Like It*, Shakespeare complicates the pattern of pastoral by critiquing not only the world of the cultured elites, but also the fantasy of escaping it and finding a better world among the woods and trees. For Alpers, the way that shepherds live becomes, in pastoral, a way of exploring the range of situations — ethical, social, erotic, poetic, economic, and others — that humans find as their common lot. Some assumptions are necessary for this to work. The first is that there really are situations of common concern to all people, whether they experience them or only imagine them. The second, as Empson notes, is that the lives of shepherds are able to capture this shared core of human experiences, "that you can say everything about complex people by a complete consideration of simple people," and that thus somehow pastoral can serve as a model for the variety of human life in all its diversity (an additional unstated assumption about pastoral here, of course, is that shepherds are simple and courtiers are complex). Generally, pastoral can assume this because it imagines that shepherds are somehow at an earlier stage of development — they live in a protracted childhood or in some noble past, possessing a kind of directness or purity that their more sophisticated descendants have lost but can dimly recall. In other words, pastoral must take for granted that there is something representative about the lives of its shepherds, that their experiences can speak to anybody, in a way that, say, the experiences of artisans or aristocrats or merchants or servants or pirates do not. *As You Like It* repeatedly questions just how representative, and indeed, how happy or easy, the shepherd's life is.

The exiled Duke is one figure who gives a voice to what we might call a pastoral view of pastoral, that is, a monocular view of pastoral. For him, exile in Arden is just a return to a simpler, better, more natural way of living. When he asks, "Are not these woods / More free from peril than the envious court?" (2.1.3–4), it is scarcely a question for him. What Arden shows him is the "good in every thing" (2.1.17). Even the Duke, though, acknowledges that his delight in his new condition did not come at once; "old custom" — that is, force of habit, and not immediate pleasure — "made this life more sweet / Than that of painted pomp" (2.1.2–3). Arden is not Club Med. It is closer to Outward Bound. What the Duke prefers about life in Arden is not its pleasantness but how its hardness is not dissembled: when the icy winter wind "bites and blows upon my body / Even till I shrink with cold, I smile and say: / This is no flattery" (2.1.8–10). Corin is no less "content with my harm" than is the Duke with his (3.2.72), but he is more forthright about the want in which he lives when Ganymede appeals to him for food:

> My master is of churlish disposition
> And little recks to find the way to heaven
> By doing deeds of hospitality....
> By reason of his absence, there is nothing
> That you will feed on. (2.4.79–85)

The shepherd's life is not as easy as pastoral convention imagines. But Corin also does not imagine the world as either flattering or not. It is simply where he lives, as he explains to Touchstone:

> Sir, I am a true labourer: I earn that I eat, get that I wear; owe no man hate, envy no man's happiness, glad of other men's good, content with my harm; and the greatest of my pride is to see my ewes graze and my lambs suck. (3.2.70–74)

Let be. In its own way, this is as limiting as the Duke's view. Where the Duke finds a single, simple message in Arden, Corin sees nothing more than life itself, brooking no alternative.

To be sure, Corin's problems, and those of his guests, are readily solved when Celia offers to buy his cottage and flocks, and the exiled Duke is able to find "good in every thing," even the "winter and rough weather" (2.5.39). But these glimpses of a less idealized pastoral world in *As You Like It* — one that is not content simply to stand in for other problems but has particular ones all its own, like bad economies and bad weather — can also open a second perspective on its world. When Corin reminds Touchstone of the dirty truth that shepherds' hands "are greasy... often tarred over with surgery of our sheep," while "[t]he courtier's hands are perfumed with civet" (3.2.51–61), Touchstone responds by noting that neither is the world of the court as clean as Corin imagines: "Civet is of a baser birth than tar, the very uncleanly flux of a cat" (3.2.64–65). There is another doubling of perspective when Silvius courts Phoebe, in high and desperate Petrarchan style, and Ganymede points out his silliness. We can see both Silvius's naïveté in executing the conventions of unrequited love by rote, and Ganymede's recognition that there are other, perhaps more sensible ways of behaving: "'Tis not her glass but you that flatters her" (3.5.55). In their different ways, and from their different points of view, Corin and Touchstone and Ganymede all direct those they speak with to see distinctions among ways the world can be represented, in a poem or in a mirror, with or without tar or civet.

It would be satisfying to see one of these ways of looking at the world as "realistic" or truer and one as falser — misguided, ideologically loaded, uninformed, even mendacious. But the relentless contrarianism of Touchstone, denying both sides their privilege, complicates settling views into a neat hierarchy. Courtiers are wrong to fantasize that shepherds are clean when in fact they are dirty, but then, courtiers are dirty themselves. As Touchstone will shortly explain to Audrey, "[T]he truest poetry is the most feigning" (3.3.17–18). In *As You Like It,* notably, both perspectives on the idealism of pastoral are given directly within the play; while the audience can flatter itself that it sees more than some of the characters, others seem to be as aware as any audience of the artifice of their world.

The double perspective of pastoral is perhaps clearest in scenes with Touchstone, and none more than that in which Corin talks to him about his new life. Touchstone is of two minds, or at least two vocabularies:

> Truly, shepherd, in respect of itself, it is a good life; but in respect that it is a shepherd's life, it is naught. In respect that it is solitary, I like it very well; but in respect that it is private, it is a very vile life. Now in respect it is in the fields, it pleaseth me well; but in respect it is not in the court, it is tedious. As it is a spare life, look you, it fits

> my humor well; but as there is no more plenty in it, it goes much against my stomach. (3.2.13–20)

This is more than just a case of Hamlet's observation that "[t]here is nothing either good or bad but thinking makes it so." What Touchstone's conversation with Corin, and really with himself, shows is how the presence of another possibility changes the meaning of what had been given. The life Touchstone lives in Arden is a good one, until he thinks about the lives he is not living because he is in Arden. It is fine to be solitary until one sees that it is private — not only the opposite of a communal, public life, but etymologically one that has been deprived of something. And so with the other conditions Touchstone sees, each of which degrades when he sees that it is susceptible to another way of seeing it. This is pastoral turned inside out, or perhaps opened up and exposed to full view: an anti-pastoral that serves to pose an alternative to what is given, and, merely by so doing, change how it can be seen, imagined, and valued.

9

What does Jaques mean when he says, "All the world's a stage"?

All the world's a stage,
And all the men and women merely players:
They have their exits and their entrances;
And one man in his time plays many parts,
His acts being seven ages. At first the infant,
Mewling and puking in the nurse's arms.
And then the whining school-boy, with his satchel
And shining morning face, creeping like snail
Unwillingly to school. And then the lover,
Sighing like furnace, with a woeful ballad
Made to his mistress' eyebrow. Then a soldier,
Full of strange oaths and bearded like the pard,
Jealous in honour, sudden and quick in quarrel,
Seeking the bubble reputation
Even in the cannon's mouth. And then the justice,
In fair round belly with good capon lined,
With eyes severe and beard of formal cut,
Full of wise saws and modern instances;
And so he plays his part. The sixth age shifts
Into the lean and slipper'd pantaloon,
With spectacles on nose and pouch on side,

> His youthful hose, well saved, a world too wide
> For his shrunk shank; and his big manly voice,
> Turning again toward childish treble, pipes
> And whistles in his sound. Last scene of all,
> That ends this strange eventful history,
> Is second childishness and mere oblivion,
> *Sans* teeth, *sans* eyes, *sans* taste, *sans* everything. (2.7.140–67)

This is one of several passages in Shakespeare's plays that are sometimes taken to be some kind of artist's statement, telling us what Shakespeare thought was the art of theater. Others include Hamlet's advice to the players about "the purpose of playing" ("to hold as 'twere, the mirror up to nature; to show virtue her own feature, scorn her own image, and the very age and body of the time his form and pressure" [3.2.20–24]) and Prospero's description of his art ("Our revels now are ended. These our actors ... / Are melted into air, into thin air" [4.1.149–50]). Sentiments similar to Jaques's here appear elsewhere in Shakespeare's plays. In *The Merchant of Venice,* Antonio, the merchant, tells a friend that the world is "A stage where every man must play a part, / And mine a sad one" (1.1.78–79); King Lear calls it "this great stage of fools" (4.6.178–79); and, even more grimly, Macbeth declares, "Life's but a walking shadow, a poor player/ That struts and frets his hour upon the stage" (5.5.24–25).

Perhaps Jaques's words, or Hamlet's, or Prospero's, are what Shakespeare believed about theater. But we should proceed with caution. In the context of these plays, these are first of all pronouncements made by particular characters in particular contexts, with their own outlooks and reasons for the descriptions they give. These are indeed claims about the powers and limits of performance and theater, but they may not tell us what *Shakespeare* thought about theater or about life. Jaques's lines in particular are so familiar, so often quoted in part and outside of their context, that it is worth looking at them more fully and closely.

Notably, Jaques is not trying to say anything in particular about stages or playing; he is using what he takes to be obvious truths about playing to explain something about ordinary life, and this in turn suggests something of how he sees playing. The stage may be able to show all the world, but that is not what interests Jaques. He is responding to the exiled Duke, who is busy moralizing Orlando for the courtiers who have accompanied him, as earlier Jaques had moralized the stag. As far as the Duke is concerned, Orlando is a valuable reminder that he and his men are not the only ones in the world who are suffering:

> [W]e are not all alone unhappy.
> This wide and universal theater
> Presents more woeful pageants than the scene
> Wherein we play in. (2.7.137–40)

Jaques takes up the Duke's theatrical metaphor and runs with it.

The idea that all the world's a stage is not new with the Duke or Jaques or even Shakespeare. Called the trope of the *theatrum mundi,* Latin for "theater of the world," it was a commonplace of thinking in the sixteenth and seventeenth centuries, and appears in classical and medieval writings as well. For a long time, scholars believed that the Globe playhouse had the related motto *Totus mundus agit histrionem* ("The whole world plays the actor," but often translated with Jaques's words, "All the world's a stage"). This is probably wrong, but the ease with which the earliest historians of the theater in the eighteenth century accepted it suggests how prevalent the notion was. It may be true, though, that *As You Like It* was the first play performed at the Globe; if so, Jaques's lines, like Hamlet's later promise to remember his father "whiles memory holds a seat / In this distracted globe" (1.5.96–97), might have set the play's first audiences glancing around them at the Globe they were in, the smaller Globe within, and representing, the larger one.

The trope of the "theater of the world" was generally used to imply one of two things. Most often it suggested the emptiness and folly of taking human life too seriously — of forgetting that, from the perspective of eternity, what we experience in this world was nothing but a kind of stage-play. Macbeth takes up an unusually grim aspect of this kind of *theatrum mundi* when he compares life to "a poor player / That struts and frets his hour upon the stage / And then is heard no more" (5.5.25–27). For Macbeth, the exit does not enter onto some greater truth, however humbling, but onto oblivion. Wisdom in this theater of the world is knowing the staginess of what others call life, and in being able to keep a cool distance from it.

But there was another sense to the *theatrum mundi,* which served as a reminder not of the greater reality that lay outside the meaningless bustle of this world, but of the need to take them seriously nevertheless — a reminder that, however much all the world was a stage, there was no place to stand outside it and pass judgment. This is closer to Antonio's sense in *The Merchant of Venice* that "every man must play a part" (1.1.78). What makes life like a performance in this vision is not that it is unreal or that it is changeable — in both cases compared to something imagined as more real, more lasting, more fixed. It is that life must be actively lived as one thing or another, that it demands effort and care to do well, and that only to do less — to hang back from living, to be a spectator rather than an actor of life — is real moral failure. As Francis Bacon put it, "in this theater of man's life, it is reserved only for God and angels to be lookers on."

Despite his eloquence, it is hard to know exactly what Jaques wants to say here. On the one hand, the step-by-step aging process Jaques describes in the Seven Ages of Man, a commonplace in its own right, does not really allow for *acting* in any sense of the word. Jaques's world, and stage, doesn't involve pretense, performance, or even real activity. You can hardly decide to be a swashbuckling soldier if you're a mopey schoolboy or a doddering oldster. You can't skip a step, go out of order, or even linger in place. You more or less just show up and await what happens. As C.L. Barber observed, Jaques is elaborating on the conclusion of Touchstone that so delighted him earlier: "[F]rom hour to hour we ripe and ripe, / And then from hour to hour we rot and rot" (2.7.26–27; 255f.). But, Barber notes, whereas the brilliance of Touchstone's version comes from his unexpected conclusion that nothing is preordained and there is no moral to how the world runs, Jaques reduces Touchstone's open-ended "[t]hereby hangs a tale" into the inevitability of a final reckoning, "*Sans* teeth, *sans* eyes, *sans* taste, *sans* everything." This sounds something like Macbeth, or Lear, or Antonio, but far from Touchstone's or Rosalind's speculative fiction-making or Prospero's equally melancholy but much more empowered picture of blending one's vision and one's life. Jaques isn't really interested in what can be done, much less in imagining how this life could be changed. He gives his speech as if it were mere description, uninflected by opinion: this is just the way things are, this is what life is like, don't mind me. He wants to tell it like it is.

On the other hand, while Jaques's account of life is glum enough, it is hardly as tragic as Lear's or Macbeth's visions of futility, if only because it seems devoid of high points or illusions of meaningfulness from the start, although it is pretty clearly less fun to be a baby or an old man than somewhere in the middle. So Jaques's stage is not really about watching and learning, either — even learning that playing is not all that important. Jaques follows neither of the usual uses of the *theatrum mundi* trope, neither of the "know that earthly life is not the most important thing" nor the "play your part as best you can" sort.

What makes Jaques's droopy narrative theatrical, and why he likens the world to a stage, is not that it is *performed* better or worse, nor that by *observing* it one can learn its vanity. For Jaques, what makes the world a stage is its reduction to spectacle rather than its opportunities for acting or action. He watches it here without feeling like he is part of it. Jaques's stage is weirdly like television. All the world may be a stage, but Jaques feels himself as excluded from it as the wounded stag from his herd. Like the Duke with his tongues in trees and books in brooks, Jaques sees life as something that will speak to him rather than something he will take part in. Telling it like it is, for Jaques, seems to require neither understanding nor responding, but a kind of battered acceptance (and perhaps a certain smugness in it, too).

There are some oversights in Jaques's squint-eyed vision that let the audience see that he is not as sharp as he thinks. For one thing, he offers a life experience like what he expects for himself, as a man of relative prosperity, as an index to all human experience. (Here we might think of how pastoral is called on to present a "representative" human life — the life that we all share, that makes us all human, duke to dustman, cat to king). He has nothing to say about how a woman's life might differ from the man's life he relates, or that of one of the inhabitants of Arden, or a servant like Adam, whom Orlando will bring onstage just as Jaques describes the final outcome of life, "mere oblivion, / *Sans* teeth, *sans* eyes, *sans* taste, *sans* everything." Where Jaques is quite ready to put himself into the place of the wounded deer, he does not seem quite as able to imagine other ways of human life, even when he is looking at strong counterexamples to his sour rehearsal. Adam, for instance, is old and weak, but hardly seems to have disappeared into "mere oblivion." He offers one of the play's strong moral models of loyalty, and is loved and protected by Orlando.

Jaques's inability to really imagine a life lived in any way other than the most obvious one — the inability to imagine a choice in how one's life was lived — is what makes it especially hard to figure out what he means by this speech. It is, in essence, a declaration of a refusal to try to live in any terms aside from the ones that one seems to have been given. Later scenes of *As You Like It* offer very different examples. For instance, Rosalind trying out the role of Ganymede, and in his guise winning Orlando not just to love her — for he loves her in a way at first glance — but to love her in a way that is not a mish-mash of romance and Petrarchan conventions, is an example of how to take the world as a stage and change how it is played upon. So is Oliver changing his mind about how to lead his life, and choosing Celia and Arden over selfishness and his estate. There are others, too. Even Touchstone's willingness to accept what he finds before him is a more careful observation, and a fuller involvement, than Jaques's finicky diagnoses.

Because he understands the stage of the world to cast him as audience and not as actor, Jaques may not mean anything by this speech. That is, he may not be doing anything by saying it but simply reciting it, as if reading it from a teleprompter. It could, in fact, be his own story, passionately and tragically told, but for him it is just a kind of general truth, although it bears every indication of being an account of his own life told without any imagination. This ambivalence or uncertainty is part of Jaques's words elsewhere in the play as well. He weeps and moralizes when he sees the wounded deer, but this doesn't hinder him from happily eating it, and singing about it, too. He is elated when he meets Touchstone in the forest, and begs to be able to put on motley and become a fool himself. But then he doesn't. His pleasure in Touchstone's fooling, and his dim sense of the kind of intellectual, emotional, and even physical freedom that being a fool would allow, do not include his actually being able to choose to try fooling, any more than his sympathy for the deer changes his position towards it. Jaques is richly capable of seeing other ways of being, but as unsatisfactory as he seems to find his own life, he is utterly unable, or unmotivated, to opt for any of them.

At the play's end, Jaques too will see that he is free to imagine, and to undertake, alternatives, when he decides to stay with the usurping Duke in Arden and take up a life of contemplation. The Jaques who would

> ... disgorge into the general world ...
> ... all the embossed sores and headed evils,
> That thou with license of free foot hast caught, (2.7.69, 67–68)

who can "suck melancholy out of a song as a weasel sucks eggs" (2.5.10–11), can do no more than recognize and reproduce his unhappiness again and again. The one who chooses at the play's end to step away from the world again and embrace a life of reflection may be subtly but powerfully different. When he chooses to remain in Arden, for the first time Jaques pushes back against the direction the world steers him in. He leaves the other characters to the lives they have chosen, and goes off to consider what life he would like to take for himself. That uncertainty in action, rather than in mere words, seems to be exactly what Jaques is in the process of coming to know. He has been (we are told) a libertine, a traveler, a social critic, finally a convertite. What will he become next? The point seems to be that Jaques's future is impossible to know — yet.

10

Why does Touchstone say the truest poetry is the most faining? Or is it "feigning"?

In his praise of Arden, the exiled Duke values above all the forest's forthrightness. Life in Arden, the Duke insists, is a lesson that speaks clearly and without deceit to those who know how to listen — those like the Duke thinks he is:

And this our life exempt from public haunt
Finds tongues in trees, books in the running brooks,
Sermons in stones and good in every thing. (2.1.15–17)

For the Duke, the forest — or really, Nature itself — is refreshingly unambiguous and briskly truthful. This is not quite what he says a few lines earlier, when he praises the climate of the forest for its honesty. For the Duke, things in the forest *speak*. A little weirdly, this viewpoint takes for granted that Nature is addressing him and his companions, as if the trees, brooks, and stones were there primarily to tell them something. A few scenes later, Orlando makes the Duke's vision comically real, when he announces that "these trees shall be my books" (3.2.5) and hangs his poems in their branches. Orlando's poetry-carving has the advantage that Orlando understands that he is the one putting the poems in the trees. The Duke seems to think that they just grow there.

When Jaques imagines the wounded stag as a wronged and abandoned citizen, the Duke enjoys it as "moralizing" — treating the world as if it had a moral or lesson for those who looked closely enough (2.1.44). He seems to have no comparable critical sense when it comes to his own translation of what the forest is saying to him. But even Orlando, although he knows that the tongues in trees are really his own, uses them to assert, like the Duke, that the world is proclaiming something. For the Duke, the world tells him of his own flawed humanity: the "counselors...feelingly persuade me what I am" (2.1.10-11). For Orlando, the message is simply the name "Rosalind": "Let no fair be kept in mind / But the fair of Rosalind" (3.2.91-92), the vacuousness of which Touchstone extends effortlessly and obscenely in the same vein:

> If a hart do lack a hind,
>   Let him seek out Rosalind
> If the cat will after kind,
>   So be sure will Rosalind ... (3.2.98-101)

"It is the right butter-woman's rank to market...the very false gallop of verses," (3.2.95, 110), he concludes. Both Orlando and the Duke share a fantasy that things themselves have a language that it is possible for them to overhear and interpret. This language of things simply confirms what they had decided already. Even Orlando's hanging of love poems in Arden's trees is not really original, but provided to him by a well-established convention of literary romance, including his precedent Orlando, Ariosto's. This language appears not as *poetry* (something made, from Greek *poiesis*) but as *data* (something given, from Latin, *datum*).

The theater director Declan Donnellan counterintuitively observes that

> one of the reasons that Shakespeare is a great writer is that he knows that words don't work and you have to know that words don't work before you can write properly because it's believing that words work perfectly that gets us into so much trouble.... [H]e understands both

his own limitations and the limitations of words. He understands his own dissarticulacy — if that word exists.

Dissarticulacy — if that word exists — would be something like both the inability to fit words together rightly, and the inability to fit the right words to things. If the Duke or Orlando possess it, they will never know, because they are sure that their words are not only right but natural, accurate, true, and necessary. Blindness to how words are not working is part of what turns speculating into moralizing, poetry into data: forgetting that there is a difference between letting a natural scene, a cold wind, or a wounded stag spur your thinking at new rhythms into new directions, and believing that you are not thinking on your own at all, but merely transcribing what things are saying. And what better way to authorize what you think than to insist that it is not you, after all, but the very nature of things that bears this message? The Duke and Orlando mute their own voices in order to reappear insistently as the subjects of the stories they tell. It is no accident that the message that both Orlando and the exiled Duke hear the world repeating is, essentially: *Here is what is important to you* — or, as we might translate it for this play, *This is As You Like It.*

As You Like It shows repeatedly how the world neglects to give us words for itself, though we badly want to take its dictation. Such dictation extends beyond the literal language that the Duke, or Jaques, or Orlando hear, to the unspoken rules of conduct that we imagine others naturally know and follow. Orlando and Oliver, for instance, are equally baffled that the bonds of brotherhood do not invariably announce themselves to the other sibling as each imagines they should, that is, respectively, as "equality" or "primogeniture." If Arden is better at addressing us than the world at large, it may be no more than that it speaks with more voices, and not always in concert. But even in Arden the world does not describe itself and what it is is not ever simply given to its visitors. Language is something humans must make for themselves, poetically, and then it can both guide and beguile. Donnellan is certainly right that words cannot do everything we want them to. The play also shows, repeatedly, how language does not match up to the world, and how this is both a kind of failure and the source of its power. Because words and worlds do not fit, because they are disarticulate, there is room to ask "what if."

"The truest poetrie," explains Touchstone to Audrey, "is the most faining" (3.3.16–17). That, at least, is what the earliest printed edition of *As You Like It* thinks he says. Beginning with Nicholas Rowe, Shakespeare's first "editor" in the modern sense of the word, it has frequently been emended to "feigning," probably better to match the rest of Touchstone's explanation:

> [A]nd Lovers are given to Poetrie: and what they sweare in Poetrie, may be said as Lovers, they do feigne. (3.3.18–19)

I'm copying the folio text scrupulously here, since not only the spelling but the syntax is difficult to understand, and "when a mans verses cannot be understood, nor a mans good wit seconded with the forward childe, understanding: it strikes a man more dead than a great reckoning in a little roome" (3.3.10–13). (Whatever that means. Scholars largely agree that the great reckoning in a little room recalls Christopher Marlowe, murdered supposedly in a fight over a check — a reckoning — in a back room of a bar ... but what of the rest of it?) More accurately, like "faining" or "feigning," Touchstone's other words gesture in more than one direction without resolving clearly into any. Do we need to add a word to make sense of it, as some modern texts do: "[W]hat they swear in poetry, [it] may be said as lovers, they do feign"? Should we contrast the swearing of poetry to the saying of lovers, for instance, and see "they do feigne" as the lovers' translation of whatever is sworn in poetry? A solid meaning seems tantalizingly near, but not quite graspable.

"Faining" means *wanting, desiring*; "feigning" means *pretending*. William Empson calls the pun "common" and points out that Shakespeare used it elsewhere, for instance, in *A Midsummer Night's Dream* when the crotchety father Egeon complains that a young man has sung to his daughter, "With faining voice, verses of faining love" (1.1.31). But of course, in a performance, there is no need to choose one or the other; they sound exactly alike. What Touchstone's words suggest is that the truest poetry most *desires* the things it reaches towards. It also most *dissembles* them. And Touchstone's *truest* is hardly more stable than his *feigning*. *True* can mean, most familiarly, *accurate*. In Shakespeare's time, it can mean *honest* — and then *truest* poetry might just be poetry that knows and tells its own *feigning*, or *faining*. *True* can also mean *unerring* or *exactly apt*, like an aim: "truest poetry" might then be the poetry best fitted to its task of feigning, or faining. Perhaps "truest poetry" is most *constant*, like a lover, more even than the things it bespeaks — by feigning (dissembling its object, because of the intensity of its desires) it would become more true (more fixed, more stable). The Duke and Orlando both speak the language of faining. But they do not see that they also speak a language of feigning — no surprises in poetry for the Duke or Orlando — and, because of that, perhaps cannot speak the truest poetry.

I will not pretend to be able to resolve the branching complexities and possibilities that Touchstone's claim opens; I am not sure if they can be resolved without turning the poetry into data, and I also do not really want to see them settled. I do not know if what Touchstone says to Audrey is itself "truest poetry," or even if it can indicate truest poetry. I want to show how the harder we try to understand these lines to say one certain thing about how things are, the more prodigally they splinter into competing possibilities. The more we try to make them about something fixed, the more things they are about and the more they say about those things. What I sense in these lines is that they lie at another pole from the Duke's speaking world or Orlando's predictable poetizing, which both must be as they are. They loosen themselves from the world and they show that disarticulation. It is *because* language does not fully catch the world (and is not fully caught by it) that through it people can shape alternatives to the world, other ways the world could be. The real powers of words do not come from their capacity to show how the world is, but to show how it is not what it is, and by thus adding to it, to change it, however blindly or incompletely.

11

What happens when Ganymede dresses as a girl?

Rosalind is far from the only female character who dresses as a man on the Shakespearean stage. Michael Shapiro counts eighty examples of crossdressing in plays during the years that the public playhouses were open (that is, in about a tenth of the total number of plays still extant), and nearly a fifth of Shakespeare's plays include women disguised as men. Why might this be?

In Shakespeare's theater, the roles of women were taken by boys (although this category seems to have included young men as old as in their twenties). In light of the enthusiastic endorsement of boy players, it seems a particularly blinkered kind of theatrical naturalism to suggest that the boy actors were just more comfortable playing boys onstage — and what, then, of Celia, who chooses the woman's part of Aliena as her disguise? (There is an element of crossdressing, or perhaps uncrossdressing, in Celia's disguise as well as Rosalind's. To become the "poor and mean" Aliena, Celia will "with a kind of umber smirch my face" [1.3.108–9]. To play female characters, boys wore a thick white make-up; rather than putting on umber to darken his face as Aliena, the boy playing Celia could simply have wiped off the white foundation, letting his natural skin color show.) In the eighteenth and nineteenth centuries, many of Shakespeare's crossdressing plays were embraced by women actors, and new "breeches parts" in plays and adaptations were written for them, in part to titillate audiences by giving them opportunities to see women actors' bodies in short or form-fitting men's clothing. But seeing a woman's legs cannot be the motive in the Elizabethan theater. If a shiver of desire attended the character of a young woman dressed as a young man, it was not simply because it gave audiences a chance to glimpse a limb they might not otherwise see.

In fact, Elizabethan audiences seem to have been much less interested in the erotics of a peekaboo sexuality than more recent audiences. At least, they don't seem to have required it. The boy actors seem explicitly to have attracted erotic attention for their own sake, as boys. Contemporary playwright and pamphleteer Thomas Middleton described the boys' company at Blackfriars as "a nest of boys able to ravish a man," which certainly sounds racy, and in the epilogue of *As You Like It*, the boy actor playing Rosalind unabashedly flirts with just about every category of body in the audience. Elizabethan culture, as Stephen Orgel notes, did not share our contemporary sense that most people screen possible objects of sexual desire first on the basis of their gender: "[N]either homosexuality nor heterosexuality existed as categories for the Renaissance mind." In that different ecology of desire, it was widely taken for granted that boys were sexually attractive to both men and women, and that men — of course the principal interest of most Elizabethan writing — were likely attracted to both women and boys. Women and boys were, to begin with, understood to be more similar than different. Rosalind can become Ganymede partly because she is "more than common tall" (1.3.112), apparently, but Ganymede can represent Rosalind so easily for Orlando because "boys and women are for the most part cattle of this color," that is, changeable and shallow compared to men, "full of tears, full of smiles, for every passion something and for no passion truly anything" (3.2.394–96). Whatever reservations about the proposed talking cure that Orlando voices, they have nothing to do with Ganymede's maleness or his ability to adequately act like Rosalind. In many plays, the convention of having boys play women's parts seems to have been little more than a kind of background noise; many plays do little to call attention to it. This can perhaps suggest how thoroughly unremarkable, even invisible, the convention could be on the Shakespearean stage. But plays that call for a female character to crossdress as a male (and while it is probably not possible to guess what fraction of plays did, but it was clearly high) foreground the convention, worry it, and call attention to its distance from lived experience.

This attractive ambiguity reaches further than most viewers initially recognize. Rosalind and Orlando are not the only ones who toy with the erotics of gender confusion. Celia's "besmirched" face may hint at boyishness, as I suggested. Oliver's rescue from the snake and the lion has a touch of a damsel in distress about it (4.3). Touchstone's courtship of Audrey seems fairly uncomplicated in terms of gender, even stereotyped in his certainty that Audrey will in time take another lover and cuckold him (3.3). But earlier in the play he remembers courting a Jane Smile in ways that suggest some sort of sexual doubleness or duplicity. "I broke my sword upon a stone," he begins (2.4.44). "Stones" was slang for *testicles,* in which case Touchstone's (there it is again!) phallic sword is knocking against another masculine organ. What else do we know of this relationship? Touchstone remembers "kissing of her batler" (2.4.46), wooing a peascod in her stead, and asking her to wear two cods from it "for my sake" (2.4.50). A batler is literally a small baton that might be used to churn butter or to beat laundry, but also suggests another small, hard tool, for instance, a penis. Wooing a peascod instead of Jane looks ahead to Orlando's misplaced wooing of Ganymede / Rosalind, but "cods" are also testicles, and "peascod" punningly inverts "codpiece," a kind of stuffed pouch that went in the front of the pants and was sometimes worn by men of the Renaissance to show off and exaggerate their genital bulge. In *Twelfth Night,* Shakespeare makes "peascod" shorthand for male maturity; in that play, the protagonist Viola, crossdressed as the young man or perhaps eunuch Cesario, is snippily described by another character as a squash that is not yet a peascod — literally the shell of a pea before the peas in it have grown, and thus figuratively a boy that has not yet developed into a man, with a glance again at the full scrotum as a sign of adult masculinity. Unlike the supposedly immature young man (because she is in fact a young woman) Viola, Jane is like a plump (or stiff?) peascod rather than a slim squash; in any case, Touchstone seems to want her to wear something that will serve as cods or testicles. In Touchstone's happy memory, Jane's body may already be equipped with a penis and testicles, or it may just be that Touchstone is interested in taking her batler and two cods as stand-ins for them. The attributes of Touchstone's fondly-remembered Jane, then, are ambiguous, or even excessive, offering in language *both/and* rather than *either/or*.

Jan Kott, who vitalized twentieth-century performances and critics alike with the dark vision of his *Shakespeare Our Contemporary*, suggested that crossdressing in *As You Like It* could be seen as a utopian vision of free desire, undetermined by its object, "an attempt at eroticism free from the limitations of the body ... a dream of love free from the limitations of sex." But in his presentism, Kott overlooks that the fantasy of crossdressing as desire unlimited by the qualities of the sexed body that he sees in *As You Like It* was built, at least in its first performances, on a reality of crossdressing, which multiplied the "limitations" and affordances of a body's sex rather than peeling them away. Kott is certainly right that the sexually indeterminate figures of *As You Like It*, the play reminds us repeatedly, are attractive. But what attracts in *As You Like It* are not bodies without markers of gender, but bodies overmarked by sexes and genders in contradictory and titillating profusion. In a 2009 production at Shakespeare's Globe, Naomi Frederick's disguised Rosalind did not seem to fool anybody for long, except Orlando, whose mind was clearly so intent on his dreams of Rosalind that he didn't notice he was talking to a girl in pants. In the Globe production, it was clear that much of her interest to the other inhabitants of Arden was the indeterminacy of her identity and the conflicting signals she was sending between a woman's body and a man's bearing.

Shakespeare seems to have written his boys' parts to accentuate this exciting doubleness, or what Phyllis Rackin calls "ambivalence." Stephen Orgel, for example, notices that in the original texts when Hymen comes to confirm the marriage of Orlando and Rosalind, he offers to "join his hand with his" — both Rosalind and Orlando are referred to with a male pronoun. Modern editors, perhaps more circumspect or more committed to ideas of consistency, almost invariably emend to "her hand" and include a stage direction for Rosalind to appear undisguised. Rackin argues that Shakespeare is more reluctant than most of his contemporary playwrights to confine his crossdressed heroines to one gender or another. One precursor drama, John Lyly's *Gallathea,* brings together two female protagonists disguised as boys. Mutually mistaking each other's gender, they fall in love — but the play ends with the miraculous transformation of one of them into a real boy, and they are free to marry. In the complicated plot of Ben Jonson's later *Epicoene,* a husband reluctantly takes a wife who at the play's end is revealed — unbeknownst even to the audience of the play — to have been, all along, a boy actor disguised as a woman, and the marriage is happily dissolved. In Lyly, sexual identity is as fluidly changeable as a costume; in Jonson, it is a kind of bedrock.

But Lyly and Jonson concur in dividing male cleanly from female, and in using the fixity of these states — even if that fixity can change again — to resolve their plots. "[U]nlike either Lyly or Jonson," Rackin observes, "Shakespeare refuses to dissolve the difference between the sex of the boy actor and that of the heroine he plays." *As You Like It* has, of course, a similar resolution, when Rosalind's revelation of herself as Rosalind cuts short the cascading desires and complications that her disguise as Ganymede has kindled. But as Marjorie Garber notices, Rosalind alone among Shakespeare's crossdressing heroines freely chooses her disguise, and freely chooses to maintain it. And at the play's end — to say nothing of the epilogue — the apparently discarded male identity of Ganymede has done as much to make the tidy resolution possible as the female identity of Rosalind: Ganymede has brought together Silvius and Phoebe, and, arguably, Rosalind and Orlando as well. "If Lyly and Jonson represent opposite extremes," contends Rackin, "Shakespeare occupies an ambiguous middle ground between them," clear on the lack of clarity the play depicts.

Ann Rosalind Jones and Peter Stallybrass characterize the back-and-forth play of Shakespeare's heroines between female and male as a positive "production of contradictory fixations," identifying tokens like body shape, vocal pitch, and gendered costumes and gestures that don't add up and even speak against one another. The real object of desire is not, as we tend to think nowadays, chosen because of its gender, but because it excitingly combines attributes of both sexes. As one male character in *The Roaring Girl* (1607) remarks as he kisses a girl dressed as a boy, "Methinks a woman's lip tastes well in a doublet" (Sc.8.47). The erotic flicker of performances like the boy player's of Rosalind of Ganymede of Rosalind did not lie in the possibility of seeing, as it were, the real thing, as in later breeches parts, but in multiplying and extending the layers of artifice, concealment, promise, and deception that were folded around a single body.

12

What is love?

As in most comedies from Shakespeare's time, the organizing frame of the plot of *As You Like It* is the study of love in its many varieties. Also like many of these plays, *As You Like It* supplies a number of eligible characters that must be fitted into appropriate marriages at the play's end. These characters and their marriages may be more or less sympathetic, appealing, or alarming to each other and to us. What is unusual in *As You Like It* is how different couples, and the separate individuals within the couples, exemplify different strategies for finding happiness within love. Love in *As You Like It*, in other words, is neither a single kind of thing, nor purely a matter of individual taste or passion. There are particular ways of talking and thinking and feeling about love, and the play offers a kind of road map of alternatives with which characters in the play can experiment. Their strategies for happiness echo some important notions about the nature of love that circulated in the period (and maybe still do), and their compilation in the play lets both characters and audiences evaluate them against one another.

Perhaps the most conventional of all these conventional attitudes towards love is the deadlocked Petrarchan unhappiness of Phoebe and Silvius. As in the most reductive interpretations of the tradition of love poetry deriving from Petrarch, Silvius steadily and hopelessly loves (perhaps now we would say *harasses* or *stalks*) Phoebe, who just as doggedly rejects him, although she is willing to make use of his devotion for her own purposes. Like any good Petrarchan lover, Silvius's lack of success does not discourage him; it only gets him to redouble his efforts, in exactly the same way as before and with exactly the same results. While Silvius loudly announces his suffering at every occasion, his fruitless pursuit is also, in some ways, just what he wants. When he first shows up complaining to the stolid Corin about his woes (2.4), we can tell that he doesn't really need Phoebe, he just needs an audience, whether that is Corin, Phoebe, Rosalind, Celia, or just himself. Everyone but Silvius seems to recognize how silly his excessiveness is. When he protests that Phoebe's disdainful glances are killing him, Phoebe reasonably points out that "there is no force in eyes / That can do hurt" (3.5.26–27). When he describes his devotions, Silvius asks Corin "how many actions most ridiculous" Corin engaged in when he was in love as a young man (2.4.27), as if it were a kind of stupidity contest between Corin and him. Not surprisingly, Silvius judges that he wins, but his curiously detached narration of what he is doing as he charges off, and his suggestion that being in love is a matter of comparing symptoms, undercuts his insistence that he is overcome by passion:

> [I]f thou hast not broke from company
> Abruptly as my passion now makes me,
> Thou hast not loved.
> O Phoebe, Phoebe, Phoebe! (2.4.34–37)

Oh dear. This is the same kind of repetition of conventional forms of love that Ganymede demands from Orlando, when he says that he notes "none of my uncle's marks" of "the quotidian of love upon him" (3.2.355, 351–52), or that Jaques runs away from with "Nay then, God b'wi' you an you talk in blank verse" (4.1.28–29).

Silvius's stiff self-absorption does not protect him from misery, and Phoebe's clear eyes regarding him do nothing to protect her from adopting exactly the same attitude when she first sees Ganymede and sighs a familiar line from Christopher Marlowe's archly ironic love poem *Hero and Leander,* "Dead shepherd, now I find thy saw of might: / 'Who ever loved that loved not at first sight?'" (3.5.82–83). Far from seeing love differently, Phoebe and Silvius simply occupy different sides of the same coin: unrequited lover, unmoved beloved. They discover their first sympathy when the newly-smitten Phoebe finds Silvius a good companion because she feels his longing in hers. "Why, I am sorry for thee, gentle Silvius," sighs Ganymede-struck Phoebe, then enlists Silvius to help her learn her new language and lure Ganymede, "since that thou canst talk of love so well" (3.5.86, 95). Passion this may be, but it is as much a passion for elegant poetry and overwrought emotions as for another person.

To judge from the poems to Rosalind that he hangs in the trees, Orlando has read a lot of the same books as Silvius. Love at first sight overthrows both Orlando and Rosalind, but Orlando's comical rehashing of unimaginative Petrarchism forces an audience to rethink how positively we should take such instant attraction. Sudden love is just as much a feature of the literary poses of Petrarchism as devout suffering. "But are you so much in love as your rhymes speak?" Ganymede asks Orlando (3.2.380–81). This is begging the question: the rhymes that Orlando writes and his certainty that they aim at expressing his love are exactly the problems. With their wooden pursuit of the ineffability of their object, they are a perfect example of tail-chasing conventionality, as everyone but Orlando recognizes. The "cure" for love (3.3.387–408) that Rosalind's training of Orlando aims at ("Love is merely a madness, and I tell you deserves as well a dark house and a whip as madmen do") is not to turn him from love, as she warns and as he seems to think, but to get him to include Rosalind in his love, as the Petrarchan model he shares with Silvius does not allow. To be be driven from a "mad humour of love to a living humour of madness" (3.2.400–401) means to move from passionately-held mood, or humor, to a vital, energizing passion.

One cure for Petrarchism is to de-idealize it, to bring it back to earth so that it actually notices the person it thinks it aims at rather than simply at its own careful disposition of a set of standardized gestures and actions (like hanging poetry on trees). Touchstone and Audrey provide one example of how to strip Petrarchan ideals from love. As always, Touchstone is a relentless debunker of the stories people tell themselves ("a material fool," Jaques, the other great critic in the play, calls him [3.3.29]: wise and pithy, but also clueless of anything spiritual). Lovers like Orlando are "given to poetry," but for Touchstone "the truest poetry is the most feigning" (3.3.17–18). Audrey's responses to Touchstone's topsy-turvy explanations, on the other hand, seem utterly sincere and utterly banal. Their scenes together, tirelessly speaking past one another, deflate just about any ideals of love one could hold, beyond "wedlock will be nibbling" (3.3.75). Touchstone's relentlessly instrumental wrenching of sense shows the Machiavellian face in the Petrarchan mask, turning its beloved into a mere opportunity for the lover to exercise his emotions. At the other pole, Audrey's embrace of a more earnest, differently conventional kind of love seems almost perfectly empty of thought or even feeling. Either way, with the help of Orlando and his poems, and Silvius and his moods, to express faith in love begins to look naïve at best, ruthless at worst.

Rosalind's lessons for Orlando also set themselves against the conventionality and solipsism of Petrarchism, but very differently from Touchstone's. As his name suggests, Touchstone tests the beliefs of others, but, as it also suggests, he does not come up with alternatives. Rosalind as Ganymede can and does. Ganymede's pledge to treat Orlando like he did his pretended former suitor, "now like him, now loath him; then entertain him, then forswear him; now weep for him, then spit at him" (3.2.398–400), zeroes in on other problems with Orlando's approach beyond its unimaginativeness — he gives up to despair too quickly when he is rejected, and his expectations are both too lofty and too grave. Love, Rosalind teaches him, is serious without being leaden; it must be light, sincerely and deeply felt, but with a sense of its own comedy. "There is only one thing sillier than being in love," says Mark Van Doren, "and that is thinking it is silly to be in love." Rosalind shows both how love literally takes time rather than being decided in an instant, and the grays in which life is actually experienced that lie between the black and white that Orlando already sees.

At their first appointment, Rosalind comments on how careless of time Orlando is, and she is right — he comes an hour late (4.1.38–39), leaves early for a dinner date with the Duke (4.1.165), and misses their second meeting altogether (albeit because of an injury [4.3]). True lovers, she objects, count even fractions of minutes. Rosalind, of course, earlier has shown a finely calibrated sense of "who Time ambles withal, who Time trots withal, who Time gallops withal and who he stands still withal" (3.2.300–302). But Orlando is careless of time not because he is easygoing, like Touchstone, who lets time wag in its own way "hour to hour" (2.7.26, 27), but because for Orlando time is no factor in love. He seems to think that love has been decided, once and for all, at a glance, and since it is already complete, an hour here or there matters very little. He is sure he will love Rosalind "[f]or ever and a day" (4.1.135). "Say 'a day' without the 'ever,'" Rosalind corrects him (4.1.136). The intermediary hours that Orlando skips over, day by day and moment by moment, are where life and love both take place. They are so important not because they vouch for love, anxiety, faithfulness, or anything else, but because they are the substance of any relationship, which is at every shared moment growing, dissolving, reforming, and changing. In their lesson, Orlando is nonplussed when Ganymede rejects his request for a kiss. When Ganymede declares, speaking as and for Rosalind, "Well, in her person, I say I will not have you," Orlando quits: "Then, in mine own person, I die" (4.1.84–85). Orlando thinks love must be all or nothing, kisses or death. It is this attitude of Petrarchan extremism that is the real enemy of love, the gradual tempering of one person to another rather than the once-and-for-all matching of parts. Orlando mistakes a refusal for an end, but Rosalind points out that a refusal is just a first step in a new direction: "[T]here begins new matter" (4.1.73–74) for the conversation that must go back and forth while the couple remains in the suspense of relation.

Love for Rosalind is never settled; it is always in passage. It is profoundly mortal: vulnerable and not timeless, but also not lethal, and not fatal. She remembers the same story of Hero and Leander as Phoebe did, but only to debunk it. Leander did not die for love of Hero, but from drowning: "[T]hese are all lies: men have died from time to time and worms have eaten them, but not for love" (4.1.97–99). When Orlando "protest[s] her frown might kill me," Rosalind answers, again sounding a little like Phoebe (who protests to Silvius, "Lie not, to say my eyes are murderers" [3.5.19]), "By this hand, it will not kill a fly" (4.1.101–2). Rosalind does not dismiss the claims of love, as Touchstone seems to. She puts them in their place. Love may be deep, as the Hellespont in which Leander drowned or as "the Bay of Portugal" to which Rosalind compares her feeling (4.1.196), but is not fatal. C.L. Barber is right to feel "a note almost of sadness" in this scene; "It is not sorrow that men die from time to time, but that they do not die for love, that love is not so final as romance would have it." But Barber seems to me to get the source of Rosalind's sadness backwards. Men will die, as Rosalind and Barber agree, whatever they think of love. What is sad is that the fantasy of fatal love can stand in the way of their living in love. As Stephen Greenblatt concludes, "The peculiar magic of Shakespeare's comedies is that love's preciousness and intensity are not diminished by such exposure to limits but rather enhanced." Rosalind's lesson is, finally, that love is life, a living humor, not death, and that, like life, it is always opening new possibilities as we exchange with one another — some better, some worse, none necessarily final. This opening of possibilities is what Rosalind and Orlando continually find, as they come slowly together from their first dumbstruck encounter to their marriage, and, one anticipates, beyond it.

Rosalind and Orlando play out one solution to the fantasies of Petrarchanism and their disillusionment. But there is, of course, another couple as well: Celia and Oliver. Their love is a mystery, as Orlando's questions show, and not just because it emerges offstage:

> Is't possible that on so little acquaintance you should like her? that but seeing you should love her? and loving woo? and, wooing, she should grant? and will you persever to enjoy her? (5.2.1–4)

Rosalind's explanation is no explanation at all:

> your brother and my sister no sooner met but they looked, no sooner looked but they loved, no sooner loved but they sighed, no sooner sighed but they asked one another the reason, no sooner knew the reason but they sought the remedy. (5.2.31–35)

No doubt after Orlando's awkward training this seems almost too good to be true. But only almost. For like the love Rosalind and Orlando grow towards, this one seems already to have been free of preconceptions. Coming upon each other unexpectedly, both Celia and Oliver are so transformed that they are led to take up a wholly new way of life in Arden. Perhaps the play includes them to hint that this unexplained, inexplicable, mysteriously transformative love is what the rest of us may all hope for, dream about, even if the harmony of our own loves is never so perfectly balanced nor their course so smooth.

13

What is the virtue in "if"?

As You Like It dramatizes attempts to bring the world and ways of talking about it into contact in particular through "similes" like Jaques's or "as-if" games like Touchstone's. These figures — both the rhetorical figures and the characters who prefer them — in fact seem to occupy the two poles in the spectrum of how language plays and is played in *As You Like It*. Touchstone's "if" entertains a possibility without committing to its consequences; it lets one see how different courses may play out, and abandon them if they go too far awry. Sometimes the going awry is better than what one could have hoped for. The prime case of this is Orlando's courtship of Rosalind by way of Ganymede, an "if" which its participants decide to accept as "is" at its end. "If" does not lose itself in its fictions, any more than Rosalind loses herself in Ganymede (or Ganymede in Rosalind) for either of Rosalind's weddings (4.1 and 5.4). "If" offers something and takes it back; as used by Jaques, "like" takes something given and pushes it further. For instance, Rosalind proposes that because she is "more than common tall," she can then "suit [both *dress* and *fashion*] me all points like a man" (1.3.112–13). Her unusual height leads Rosalind to imagine a new gender.

Both figures have attendant risks. "If" can decay into idle dreaming or nonsense, as when Celia swears for herself and Rosalind "by our beards, if we had them" (1.2.72). More seriously, "like" can forget and mistake itself for "is," as the Duke does when he listens to the trees or Jaques does when he declares that all the world's a stage. "While there may be much virtue in 'If' (5.4.103)," Robert Watson points out, "in 'Like' there lies the temptation to a great sin, an appropriative violence; 'If' may be a 'peacemaker,' but 'like' is a gesture of conquest." Watson perhaps overstates the stakes of "like," at least in *As You Like It*. The "appropriative violence" in "like" is potential, not necessary; *if* "like" mistakes itself for "is," that violence erupts as surely as the duel that Touchstone avoids, if not as dramatically—but only *if*. Tellingly, though, the characters most prone to the forgetful "gesture of conquest" in "like" are privileged men, the Duke, Jaques, and Orlando. Marjorie Garber, a scholar of both Shakespeare and of transvestism, points out that Rosalind's invisibility follows from Orlando's preoccupation with notions about love and is one of the things Orlando needs to unlearn; although in his poetry Orlando bids, "Let no face be kept in mind / But the fair of Rosalind" (but to whom, exactly? This is symptomatic of Orlando's poetry problem), he doesn't recognize her when he sees her. Orlando believes he can love Rosalind without needing to listen to what she has to say, because he can already frame her in similes.

Touchstone's discussion of the virtue of "if" late in the play articulates what the play has shown. Tellingly, he addresses it to Jaques, the character who most needs to hear it. Touchstone vouches for himself as a courtier:

> I have trod a measure; I have flattered a lady; I have been politic with my friend, smooth with mine enemy; I have undone three tailors; I have had four quarrels and like to have fought one. (5.4.44–47)

Maneuvering through the hazards of grammatical mood as adventurously as any duelist, Touchstone evades what seems like an inescapable insult and the duel that follows it:

> I knew when seven justices could not take up [that is, resolve] a quarrel, but when the parties were met themselves, one of them

thought but of an "if," as, "If you said so, then I said so;" and they shook hands and swore brothers. (5.4.96–100)

"*Like* to have fought" yields to "*If* you said…." "Your 'if,'" concludes Touchstone, "is the only peacemaker: much virtue in 'if'" (5.4.100–101).

The "virtue in 'if'" inverts the forthrightness of the Duke's legible brooks and chatty trees as if in a mirror. It grants words a tremendous power, but only insofar as they are also vulnerable, tentative, literally revocable. Words cannot remake the world, nor does the world simply make them, as the Duke imagines. Because the world and words are disarticulate, words work, but not perfectly. But because under "if" they are not expected to work perfectly or permanently, they do work. As if to test Touchstone's hypotheses, the play hurries towards its conclusion in a whirlwind of "ifs," most of them Rosalind's ("ands" and "buts" are mine), pointing in different directions:

> [to Silvius] I will help you, if I can [*and she can*]. [to Phoebe] I would love you, if I could [*but she cannot*]. — To-morrow meet me all together. (5.2.106–8)

Sometimes "if" means yes; sometimes it means no. This gets even more complicated when Rosalind presents what look like factually true consequences for possible antecedents:

> [to Phoebe] I will marry you, if ever I marry woman, and I'll be married to-morrow. [to Orlando] I will satisfy you, if ever I satisfied man, and you shall be married to-morrow. (5.2.106–11)

Later and more compactly,

> [to Orlando] I'll have no husband, if you be not he [*but you are, and I will*]. [to Phoebe] Nor ne'er wed woman, if you be not she [*and you are, but I will not*]. (5.4.121–22)

The world can confirm the experiment of an "'if'" or negate it, but in the epilogue, Rosalind shows how "if" and "is," word and world, poetry and data, simply spin independently of each other:

> If it be true that good wine needs no bush [*but is it true?*], 'tis true that a good play needs no epilogue; yet to good wine they do use good bushes, and good plays prove the better by the help of good epilogues. (Epilogue.3–6)

In other words, good wine needs no bush, but sometimes it has one anyway. Sometimes it doesn't. What the bush says does not tell us how the wine tastes. Only trying it can tell that.

14

What happens in the epilogue?

As we expected — although probably not how we expected — *As You Like It* resolves the pitfalls and obstacles the play has carefully laid for itself and gives us a happy ending. The couples Rosalind and Orlando, Celia and Oliver, Phoebe and Silvius, and Audrey and Touchstone are suitably distributed; the exiled Duke is restored to his throne; the inevitable singleton Jaques acknowledges that he is "for other than for dancing measures" (5.4.191) and chooses to remain in Arden, ostensibly to learn from the conversion of the usurping former Duke, but in any case out of the way of the lovers who are set to return to their reconstituted worlds of court and forest. In parallel benedictions, the seemingly contrary principles of Hymen (5.4.129–34), the pagan god of marriage who brings things together, and Jaques (5.4.184–90), who becomes almost a spirit of solitude and self-sufficiency, bless one by one all those who are entering into their new futures together. Hymen, appropriately, offers a word to each couple:

> You and you no cross shall part
> You and you are heart in heart … (5.4.129–30)

(and so forth), while Jaques speaks only to each of the males:

> You to your former honour I bequeath ...
> You to a love that your true faith doth merit; (5.4.184, 186)

As Hymen promises, "earthly things made even / Atone together" (5.4.106–7). The Duke hurries the new dispensation forward to its conclusion in pleasure:

> Proceed, proceed! We'll begin these rites
> As we do trust they'll end, in true delights. (5.4.195–96)

As You Like It begins, like so many comedies of Shakespeare's time, in discontent and disorder, but at the end it seems to reach the moment at which all have what they like. The play has advanced from a multiplicity of discords to shared harmony, even as the Duke pledges that the "rites" the play ends with — both the marriages and the ritual of performance, applause, exit — restore some imagined prior harmony, circling back to end in a "delight" that they emerged from. It seems to be an image of perfect closure.

But the play does not end here, and when everyone else dances out Rosalind remains onstage. It's hard not to feel a little unbalanced here as the "things made even" begin to tilt again. Everything seemed, surprisingly, to have been sewn up; now, surprisingly, something seems to be left over again. Rosalind is not "At-one together" (to play with Hymen's phrase), but all alone. In the epilogue she also becomes more than one.

Rosalind's epilogue is the play's last experiment in how things can be otherwise than they are, and how they can return to what they are, changed. An epilogue for which an actor stepped out of character to ask for applause was an established way to end an Elizabethan play. But as Rosalind makes clear, her epilogue draws on this stage convention without really disappearing into it. "It is not the fashion," she begins, "to see the lady the epilogue" (Epilogue.1), but there Rosalind is. We do not see her for long. As Rosalind speaks, she sheds one identity after another. In the play, she laid aside Rosalind for Ganymede and then Ganymede for Rosalind: now she cycles quickly through "lady" (Epilogue.1), epilogue-speaker (Epilogue.2), one "not furnished like a beggar" (Epilogue.9), and at last a conditional "if I were a woman" (Epilogue.16–17), until the boy actor who plays her leaves the stage, alone.

Shakespeare liked this kind of long goodbye, with an actor bidding the audience and his part farewell at the same time, as if he stood at the precise joint where the real world and the world of the play intersected. We see it in the epilogues to plays like *A Midsummer Night's Dream, Twelfth Night,* and *The Tempest.* But in these cases it is the actor who has already surrendered his role who speaks and conjures applause. *As You Like It* is unique in the way Rosalind fades from view as she addresses the audience. In the epilogue Rosalind steers the attention of the audience away from her (or him?), but he (or she?) is able to do this, first of all, because she (or he?) has already captured their attention in a way that is cast as explicitly erotic, the promise of a kiss, as she peels away layers of dissimulation to the audience. For an Elizabethan audience, Rosalind's erotically-charged allure was prompted in part because her epilogue takes the place of the usually bawdy jig. But it also arises because of Ganymede-Rosalind-the boy actor's making-visible of the crossing of easily distinguished gender roles, from one gender to another, by her (or his) flirting with both sides of the audience. It is also a histrionic strip-tease, with the lure of seeing all — the real actor making the play, the reality that the play has played with "ifs" and "likes," teasingly promised and then just as teasingly withdrawn.

It is easy to think of Rosalind's transformation as a change of a "look," as if the actor would simply shift visual cues — perhaps removing a piece of woman's clothing, or adopting a different posture or tone of voice to signal a shift "out of character" even if not "out of gender." In fact, many actors do one or more of these bits of business at this point. At least as Rosalind describes it, though, what happens is a change of *desire.* To use the play's language, it is a last turning, or returning, of the question, what is it that is as you like it? In this case, the liking is explicitly an erotic one. What allows Rosalind in the epilogue to shift from identity to identity is announced as the sexual attraction between actor and audience, and within the audience. Rosalind's flickering identity — girl? boy? performer? — shows the audience that, like the characters whom they have been watching, they are caught up in experimentation about what it is that they like. Through the play they have seen, they have also been lead through a series of experiences in desire and imagination.

Rosalind's epilogue begins with the women, whom she "conjure[s]" (Epilogue.11) to like the play as much as they like "for the love you bear to the men" (Epilogue.12). The men, in turn, must like whatever is left, "for the love you bear to women" (Epilogue.14). "If I were a woman," continues the actor — no longer one at this point? — "I would kiss as many of you as had beards that pleased me" (Epilogue.16–18). "One would have thought such a thing impossible until the invention of the motion-picture camera and celluloid film," Bruce Smith brilliantly observes, comparing this moment to the overwhelming strangeness of the film close-up, through which we startlingly "get much closer to actors' faces than we ever do to faces in real life except for whispering, kissing, and/or having sex." The conjuring of proximity itself conjures an erotic charge. But this closeness is also subject to Touchstone's powerful "if," that in a single word both promises and takes away. Instead of kissing, the actor speaks and directs the audience away from the stage back towards itself. Only they are close enough to kiss, Rosalind seems to remind us.

Instead of "If I were a woman," women playing Rosalind sometimes say "If I were among you ...," making the imaginary condition only the gap between stage and reality rather than also that between genders. But either can be crossed. The actor who speaks the epilogue is no more there for kissing than Ganymede was for Orlando. But also no less. We may in fact be closer to the different Elizabethan world of playing than we initially imagine. The ecology of gender described by Stephen Orgel, in which boys are analogous to women rather than opposites, and equally desirable to men and women, may seem as foreign to us, perhaps, as pastoral. But modern audiences love Rosalind as much as we think earlier ones did. Her erotic conjuration and mixed gender messages work on us as well. The Shakespearean scholar Alfred Harbage remarked that "[m]ore critics have fallen in love with Rosalind than with any other of Shakespeare's heroines." George Bernard Shaw had noticed the same thing, and tartly concluded,

> The popularity of Rosalind is due to three main causes. First, she only speaks blank verse for a few minutes. Second, she only wears a skirt for a few minutes (and the dismal effect of the change at the end to the wedding dress ought to convert the stupidest champion of petticoats to rational dress). Third, she makes love to the man instead of waiting for the man to make love to her.

But Rosalind entrances her audience regardless of whether she is a boy playing a girl playing a boy playing a girl or a girl playing a girl playing a boy playing a girl. Numerous all-male productions of *As You Like It* staged in the late twentieth and twenty-first centuries, most influentially Cheek by Jowl's 1991 production with Adrian Lester as Rosalind, have amply shown this. These can't recreate the conditions of Shakespeare's theater, of course, because for modern audiences men playing women's roles is a novelty, not an expectation. But they have suggested some of the fascination of watching an actor carefully revealing layer upon layer of clues to identity. A recent editor of the play, Juliet Dusinberre, illuminates something of the remarkable feel of the epilogue as a kind of contest between the actor of Rosalind and Rosalind herself: "[T]he boy who has played Rosalind perhaps hardly wants to go back to being a lady. She wants to have the last word as a boy." In the epilogue, even as she fades, we may see something of what Rosalind herself — not as an actor or in a fiction, but *Rosalind as an actor* — likes.

In fact, what Rosalind actually asks in the epilogue doesn't make much sense. Instead, it calls attention to the way that "play," *liking, pleasing,* the promise of *kissing,* do the work of *meaning.* The audience is left with its own sense of what is as it likes it, and Rosalind's actor does more than hint that it isn't the play that is on the stage. "[A]s much of this play as please you ... between you and the women the play may please" (Epilogue.12–13, 15–16): Rosalind reminds the audience of the play's title, and that the play has also been for their liking, as the audience — Rosalind hopes — likes it. But "play" is also short, in Elizabethan slang, for sexual play. Rosalind has perhaps played some with us. And as individual desires begin to stir within the audience, as they play with each other rather than paying attention to the play of the actors, their varied desires are withdrawn from the actor — and he is freed to leave. The audience remains. They are now their own stage, to behold and on which to act.

15

The end?

> Shakespeare & the dream. A dream is all wrong, absurd, composite, & yet completely right: in *this* strange concoction it makes an impression. Why? I don't know. And if Shakespeare is great, as he is said to be, then we must be able to say of him: Everything is wrong, things *aren't like that* — & is all the same completely right according to a law of its own. It could be put like this too: If Shakespeare is great, then he can be so only in the whole *corpus* of his plays, which create their *own* language & world. So he is completely unrealistic. (Like the dream.)
> — Ludwig Wittgenstein (1949)

In what kind of world does the audience — do *we* — remain when Rosalind disappears? She does not leave the stage, but before our eyes vanishes from it into air, into thin air, as Shakespeare's Prospero would later describe his own theatrics. She leaves nothing of herself but lingering desires that can no longer take her as their focus. That is the beginning of an answer: where most comedies work to channel and calm desire at the end — in marriages, resolutions, celebrations — desire remains startling and moving at the end of *As You Like It*. The desires at the beginning of the play have all changed — the usurping Duke has given up his rule, the exiled Duke is apparently happy to take it back, Oliver no longer wants his rights as eldest son and heir nor

Celia her companionship with Rosalind. Even the desire that might seem most consistent — Rosalind's and Orlando's — is very different than it was. If anything, the play hints, against long habits about comedy and happy endings, that desires will continue to change, mostly happily. Rosalind leaves a world still open for desire and changes in desires.

In this quotation, Wittgenstein is not, so far as I know, speaking in particular of *As You Like It*. If anything, he seems to be arguing that breaking out *As You Like It* or any other play from the whole texture of Shakespeare's writings would somehow misprize them. But *As You Like It* presents one especially good way to approach that entire texture, because over its whole course it seems to pick up greater and greater escape velocity to carry its characters, its readers, and its audiences beyond the limits of its plot. We don't, I think, speculate about what will follow so much as feel that something will follow. Wittgenstein's great insight here is that Shakespeare's plays — and perhaps in particular *As You Like It* — follow rules of their own. What Wittgenstein notes about Shakespeare's ability to fashion worlds (not a poet but a creator of language, he calls him) is nowhere on brighter display, nor under more careful scrutiny, than in *As You Like It,* in which so many characters so self-consciously pursue their own diverging experiments in reworking the world, and onlookers — who in *As You Like It* also include the same characters — can see how these worlds unfold into new, unanticipated ones. Wittgenstein seems to imagine Shakespeare's writing as immersive, dreamlike, something in which we can unwittingly lose ourselves and find our way in only from outside, as it were, where we recognize that "things *aren't like that.*"

What *As You Like It* also suggests is that it is much harder to step outside the perspectives on the world that are opened up around us than Wittgenstein suggests here. The play notably lacks the settled, universally accepted point of view that would allow one to pronounce any other way of looking at the world as "completely unrealistic." It makes it hard to reject possible worlds just by asserting "things *aren't like that."* The play's most foolish mistakes come from exactly such fatalistic, resigned, and, in the long run, shortsighted ways of seeing the world just as it is (at least in *As You Like It* they are shown to be fatalistic!). In *As You Like It* things neither aren't like that nor are like that, we might say — because we cannot determine the *that*. Things are not data simply given to us immutably and monovocally in one way or another. We make and remake them as we go. The happiest figures in the play are those who, in spite of the world's contradictions of what they like, imagine that things can be otherwise, and undertake to make the things that "*aren't like that*" more as they like it. Even at its conclusion, releasing its audience to itself and Rosalind to Arden, *As You Like It* resists the sense of an ending. Its promise is that because this world — whatever it may be — does not exhaust the desires that it moves us to, and because those desires will move us to ask, what if?, realizing other worlds in the world we find ourselves in will always be possible.

Notes to the Text

As originally commissioned, the citations in these essays would have been suggestive rather than precise: "George Bernard Shaw said" rather than "George Bernard Shaw said... (in *Shaw on Shakespeare,* New York: Applause Books, 1989, 27)." There were to be no footnotes or endnotes. When I took the essays to the Dead Letter Office, I was tempted to keep the citations conversational. I admire the offhandedness of Montaigne, who, like most early modern writers, scarcely cites what he uses, and Barthes's casual erudition in *A Lover's Discourse,* where he coyly gestures towards his sources by their initials or a single title word in the margins. But in the end I decided to include fuller citations, in part because I owe so much to these works I've read and in part because I didn't entirely like the feeling of insiderdom that the use of allusion suggested. My compromise was not to mark the references in the essays themselves, and to tuck citations in the back of the book, where a reader can find them if he or she wants, but can also read without being interrupted by them (although I suspect academic readers feel the pull of footnotes more deeply than most others). The notes below respond to cue words in the essays, as in an early modern theatrical part, which gave each actor only a few words from the preceding speech. For those less performatively inclined, page numbers are also included.

Richard Knowles's *Variorum* edition was an indispensable treasury, especially for earlier criticism.

FOREWORD ♦ *Trying*

x "the ambiguous genre": "je n'ai produit que des essais, genre ambigu où l'écriture le dispute à l'analyse," Barthes, *Leçon*, 7.

xi the phrase appears only once in the text of his *Essais*: in the "Apologie pour Raimond Sebond," essay 2.12, p. 527 in the Villey-Saulnier edition.

xi when he notes that he bears it: Montaigne writes ambiguously, "Cette fantasie est plus securement conceve par interrogation: Que sçay-je? comme je la porte à la devise d'un balance," "This notion [of doubt] is much more surely grasped by a question, What do I know? which I bear in the device of a balance." But *porte,* or "bear," could mean to carry the device physically or simply to display it.

xi Later, annotating his own copy: on page 220 of the so-called Bordeaux copy of the *Essais,* into which Montaigne wrote his additions, second thoughts, and changes of direction. I say the medal recedes into language, but it may never actually have emerged from it: while the story of the medal is regularly repeated — it is a very good one — there seems to be no firm evidence that the medal was ever actual rather than literal, or literary. The device is mentioned by Pascal, and an image of a medal with the motto QUE SÇAY IE and the image of a balance is printed in some seventeenth-century editions of the *Essais*. But it seems to have been conflated with another medal made for Montaigne in 1576, which still exists; that one has the Greek motto *epekhō,* "I withhold," which Montaigne renders as *Je ne bouge,* "I do not move," a few pages before he asks *Que sçay-je?* See Demonet's discussion of "Jeton" in *Dictionnaire Montaigne*.

xi philosophy begins in wonder: Aristotle, *Metaphysics*, 982b.

xii   "in the emphatic essay": Adorno, "The Essay as Form," 11.
xii   it "cunningly anchors itself in texts": Adorno, "The Essay as Form," 20.

INTRODUCTION • As You Like It

15   Epigraph: "I should be disposed to choose *As You Like It*": Bradley, *Oxford Lectures on Poetry* (1909), 354.
15   "the most ideal of any of this author's plays": Hazlitt, *Characters of Shakespear's Plays* (1817), 305.
15   "Who ever failed, or could fail, as Rosalind?": Shaw, *Shaw on Shakespeare: An Anthology of Bernard Shaw's Writings on the Plays and Productions of Shakespeare*, 29.
15   "many academic critics since the 1970s … *don't* like it": Smith, *Phenomenal Shakespeare*, 5.
16   "the philosopher of the play": Van Doren, *Shakespeare*, 159.
16   "the sights and sounds of *As You Like It*": Smith, *Phenomenal Shakespeare*, 5.
18   "*As You Like It* seems written purely to please": Brook, Introduction to *As You Like It: Décor and Costumes by Salvador Dalí*, 6.

1 • *What happens in* As You Like It?

19   "what takes place is not so essential as what is said": Schlegel, *A Course of Lectures on Dramatic Art and Literature*, 2: 172–73.

2 • *What is the play about?*

29   Winnicott distinguished two ways people can think about alternative realities: in the chapters "Dreaming, Fantasying, and Living: A Case-History" and "Playing: A Theoretical Statement" from *Playing and Reality*.
30   "a common beholding place": The word *theater*, adopted from Latin, which borrowed it from Greek, first appears

in English in a Wycliffite Bible of 1384, where the unfamiliar word is glossed as a "comune biholdiyng place" (s.v. "theatre" in the electronic *Middle English Dictionary*, Regents of the University of Michigan, http://quod.lib.umich.edu/m/med/). Similar explanations of the word appear in Wynkyn de Worde's *Ortus Vocabulorum* (1500), Thomas Elyot's *Dictionary* (1538), John Baret's *Alveary* (1573), Thomas Cooper's *Thesaurus* (1584), John Rider's *Bibliotheca Scholastica* (1589), and Claude Hollyband's *Dictionary of French and English* (1593). In Chaucer's *Knight's Tale*, "circle" and "entry" appear as variants of the word *theater* in some manuscripts, suggesting that the word was unfamiliar to the copyists (s.v. "theatre," *MED*).

30 the human is most fully human in the freedom of its play: in Letter XV of Schiller's *Letters on the Aesthetic Education of the Human*. Huizinga wrote a study of play called *Homo Ludens* (1938); Piaget discusses child's play in *Play, Dreams and Imitation in Childhood* (1945).

3 • What's in a name?

34 "Rosalind is also a feigned name": from E.K.'s notes on the poem "Januarye" in Spenser's *Shepherd's Calendar*.

34 "execrable and horrible sinnes": more of E.K.'s notes on "Januarye."

34 "the most illicitly carnal of all the divine amours is translated into the most positively sanctioned": Barkan, *Transuming Passion: Ganymede and the Erotics of Humanism*, 24.

36 Where did "Orlando" come from?: Ascoli, "Wrestling with Orlando," explores the derivation from Ariosto's knightly hero.

4 • *What happens when Rosalind dresses as a boy?*

40 even the title... "places 'like' as a barrier between 'you' and 'it'": Watson, *Back to Nature: The Green and the Real in the Late Renaissance*, 77.

40 "'Like' implicates *you* in *it*": Smith, *Phenomenal Shakespeare*, 3.

43 the layers of Rosalind's disguises and roles: Jean Howard's article "Crossdressing, the Theatre, and Gender Struggle in Early Modern England" discusses the many varieties and significations of crossdressing in early modern London.

5 • *Where is Arden?*

45 "a Shakespearean myth": Dusinberre, Introduction to *As You Like It*, 50, 51.

46 "The 'If' that Shakespeare ventures": Stauffer, *Shakespeare's World of Images: The Development of His Moral Ideas*, 79.

46 the mode of "as-if"... does not lend itself to proof or disproof: Kermode, *The Sense of an Ending: Studies in the Theory of Fiction*, 39–40.

47 the "saturnalian pattern" of inversion: "The Saturnalian Pattern" is Barber's first chapter. The following quotations from Barber are taken, in order, from *Shakespeare's Festive Comedy: A Study of Dramatic Form and Its Relation to Social Custom*, 6, 7, and 9.

48 an innovation in the history of the genre of comedy: Frye, "The Argument of Comedy," 67–70.

48 "Terentian and Plautine": Barber, *Shakespeare's Festive Comedy*, 1.

49 Frye... called it the Green World: Frye, "Argument," 67.

49 "red and white": Frye, "Argument," 70.

50 Harry Berger revises Frye's notion of the Green World: In "The Renaissance Imagination: Second World and Green World," the first chapter in the collection by that name.

51   namely the Blue World: see, for instance, Mentz, "Shakespeare's Beach House."

6 • Why do we hear about what Jaques said to a deer?

55   the same as that of Narcissus: Watson, *Back to Nature*, 80–85.

55   an argument from lack of imagination: I wish I could recall where I first heard this sparkling criticism.

56   "strategic anthropomorphism": Bennett, *Vibrant Matter: A Political Ecology of Things*, 120.

7 • What does Jaques telling us about Touchstone telling time tell us about them?

60   "[H]e came to life again a century later": Dowden, *Shakespeare: A Critical Study of his Mind and Art*, 78.

60   "Hamlet *avant la lettre*": this quotation and the previous one are from Brandes, *William Shakespeare: A Critical Study*, 260, 263.

60   "so much removed…from Hamlet": Farnham, *The Shakespearean Grotesque: Its Genesis and Transformations*, 123.

8 • What is pastoral?

64   what concerns the lives of shepherds: Alpers's claim is ultimately far more involved than this, but this capacious and simple recognition lies at its core. Alpers, *What is Pastoral?*, 22.

64   a "clash between different modes of feeling": Empson, *Seven Types of Ambiguity*, 114.

64   "the real world is abstract and the unreal concrete": Iser, *The Fictive and the Imaginary: Charting Literary Anthropology*, 45.

65   "you can say everything about complex people": Empson, *Some Versions of Pastoral*, 137.

68 "nothing either good or bad": these lines appear only in the Folio, *Hamlet,* 2.2.247–48.

9 • What does Jaques mean when he says, "All the world's a stage"?

70 Hamlet's advice to the players: *Hamlet,* 3.2.20–24, punctuated here as in the Folio. The editors of the edition I cite capitalize the nouns, which makes it look to modern readers as if Hamlet is allegorizing them. Maybe — but maybe not, and there seems no particular reason to think he is.

71 This is probably wrong: as Tiffany Stern carefully argues in her article on it, "Was *Totus Mundus Agit Histrionem* ever the Motto of the Globe Theatre?"

71 Hamlet's later promise to remember his father: from the second Quarto, this time.

72 As Francis Bacon put it, "in this theater…": *De Augmentis* 7.1; V: 8, VII: 718.

72 Jaques is elaborating on the conclusion of Touchstone: Barber, *Shakespeare's Festive Comedy,* 256.

10 • Why does Touchstone say the truest poetry is the most faining? Or is it "feigning"?

79 "one of the reasons that Shakespeare is a great writer": Donnelan's interview with Peter Holland, "Directing Shakespeare's Comedies: In Conversation with Peter Holland," 162.

81 William Empson calls the pun "common": Empson, *Some Versions of Pastoral,* 137.

81 "With faining voice": I follow the earliest version here, Quarto 1. Later quartos and the folio editions have "feigning" and "faining." With comical confidence, later editors have reversed these to read "faining" and "feigning."

11 • What happens when Ganymede dresses as a girl?

83   eighty examples of crossdressing: listed in the appendix to Shapiro's *Gender in Play on the Shakespearean Stage*.

84   "a nest of boys able to ravish a man": in *Father Hubburd's Tales*, 173.

84   "neither homosexuality nor heterosexuality existed": Orgel, *Impersonations: The Performance of Gender in Shakespeare's England*, 59.

86   "an attempt at eroticism free from the limitations of the body": Kott, *Shakespeare Our Contemporary*, 273.

87   "ambivalence": Rackin, "Androgyny, Mimesis, and the Marriage of the Boy Heroine," 37, but ambivalent figures are the topic of the entire paper.

87   Rosalind and Orlando are referred to with a male pronoun: Orgel, *Impersonations*, 32–33; Masten, "Textual Deviance," 155–56, notices this moment as well, and uses it to think about the importance of holding off on rationalizing Shakespeare's texts.

87   Shakespeare is more reluctant than most: Rackin, "Androgyny," 37.

87   "[U]nlike either Lyly or Jonson": Rackin, "Androgyny," 31.

87   Rosalind alone...freely chooses her disguise: Garber, "The Education of Orlando," elaborated in the chapter on *As You Like It* in *Shakespeare After All*.

88   "Shakespeare occupies an ambiguous middle ground": Rackin, "Androgyny," 31.

88   "production of contradictory fixations": Jones and Stallybrass, *Renaissance Clothing and the Materials of Memory*, 207.

12 • What is love?

92   "There is only one thing sillier than being in love": Van Doren, *Shakespeare*, 134.

94   "A note almost of sadness": Barber, *Shakespeare's Festive Comedy*, 267.

94   "The peculiar magic of Shakespeare's comedies": Greenblatt, *Shakespeare's Freedom*, 3.

13 • *What is the virtue in "if"?*

98   "'If' may be a 'peacemaker,' but 'like' is a gesture of conquest": Watson, *Back to Nature*, 100.
98   Rosalind's invisibility follows from Orlando's preoccupation with notions about love: Garber, "The Education of Orlando."

14 • *What happens in the epilogue?*

104   "One would have thought such a thing impossible": Smith, *Phenomenal Shakespeare*, 4.
105   "More critics have fallen in love with Rosalind than with any other of Shakespeare's heroines": Harbage, *Shakespeare: A Reader's Guide*, 241.
105   "The popularity of Rosalind is due to three main causes": Shaw, *Shaw on Shakespeare*, 27.
105   "She wants to have the last word as a boy": Dusinberre, Introduction to *As You Like It*, 25.

15 • *The end?*

107   Epigraph: "Shakespeare & the dream": quoted in *Culture and Value*, 83, from Wittgenstein's 1949 notebooks.
108   not a poet but a creator of language: Wittgenstein, *Culture and Value*, 84. In German, Wittgenstein's words are even more suggestive and elusive: not a *Dichter*, by traditional (although incorrect) derivation one who condenses and intensifies — thickens — language, but a *Schöpfer*, one who makes it.

Works Cited

Adorno, Theodor. "The Essay as Form." In *Notes to Literature*, Vol. 1, edited by Rolf Tiedemann, translated by Shierry Weber Nicholson, 3–33. New York: Columbia University Press, 1991.

Alpers, Paul. *What is Pastoral?* Chicago: University of Chicago Press, 1996.

Ascoli, Albert. "Wrestling with Orlando: Chivalric Pastoral in Shakespeare's Arden." *Renaissance Drama* 36/37 (2010): 293–317.

Bacon, Francis. *Works*. Edited by James Spedding, Robert Leslie Ellis, and Douglas Denon Heath. 14 vols. London: Longman and Co., 1857–74. Facsimile Reprint. Stuttgart: Friedrich Fromann Verlag, 1963.

Barber, C.L. *Shakespeare's Festive Comedy: A Study of Dramatic Form and Its Relation to Social Custom*. 1960. Princeton: Princeton University Press, 2011.

Baret, John. *An Alvearie or triple dictionarie*. London: Henry Denham, 1573.

Barkan, Leonard. *Transuming Passion: Ganymede and the Erotics of Humanism*. Stanford: Stanford University Press, 1991.

Barthes, Roland. *Leçon. Leçon inaugurale de la Chaire de Sémiologie Littéraire du College de France*. Paris: Seuil, 1978.

Bennett, Jane. *Vibrant Matter: A Political Ecology of Things*. Durham: Duke University Press, 2010.

Berger, Harry, Jr. *Second World and Green World in Renaissance Fiction-Making.* Berkeley: University of California Press, 1990.

Bradley, A.C. *Oxford Lectures on Poetry.* 1909. London: St, Martin's Press, 1965.

Brandes, Georg. *William Shakespeare: A Critical Study.* 1895–96. Translated by William Archer, Mary Morison, and Diana White. 2 vols. London: William Heinemann, 1898.

Brook, Peter. Introduction to *As You Like It: Décor and Costumes by Salvador Dalí,* by William Shakespeare. London: Folio Society, 1953.

Burke, Kenneth. *Language as Symbolic Action: Essays on Life, Literature, and Method.* Berkeley: University of California Press, 1968.

Burckhardt, Jacob. *The Civilization of the Renaissance in Italy.* 1860. Translated by S.G.C. Middlemore. London: Phaidon Press, 1995.

Cooper, Thomas. *Thesaurus linguæ Romanae Britannicae.* London: Henry Bynneman, 1584.

Demonet, Marie-Luce. "Jeton." In *Dictionnaire Montaigne,* edited by Philippe Desan. Paris: Champion, 2004. Also available as "Le Jeton de Montaigne," www.academia.edu/8637027/Le_Jeton_de_Montaigne.

Donnellan, Declan. "Directing Shakespeare's Comedies: In Conversation with Peter Holland." *Shakespeare Survey* 56 (2003): 161–66.

Dowden, Edward. *Shakespere: A Critical Study of his Mind and Art.* 1875. New York: Harper and Brothers, 1881.

Dusinberre, Juliet, ed. Introduction to *As You Like It,* by William Shakespeare. Arden Shakespeare, 3rd edn. London: Bloomsbury, 2006.

Elyot, Thomas. *Bibliotheca Eliotae, Eliotis Librarie, This Dictionarie....* London: Thomas Berthelet, 1538.

Empson, William. *Seven Types of Ambiguity.* 1930. New York: New Directions, 1947.

Empson, William. *Some Versions of Pastoral.* 1935. New York: New Directions, 1974.

Farnham, Willard. *The Shakespearean Grotesque: Its Genesis and Transformations.* Oxford: Oxford University Press, 1971.

Frye, Northrop. *Anatomy of Criticism: Four Essays.* Princeton: Bollingen Press, 1957.

Frye, Northrop. "The Argument of Comedy." In *English Institute Essays: 1948,* edited by D.A. Robertson, Jr., 58–73. New York: Columbia University Press, 1949.

Garber, Marjorie. "The Education of Orlando." In *Comedy from Shakespeare to Sheridan,* edited by A.R. Braunmuller and James C. Bulman, 102–12. Newark: University of Delaware Press, 1986.

Garber, Marjorie. *Shakespeare After All.* New York: Pantheon, 2004.

Greenblatt, Stephen. *Shakespeare's Freedom.* Chicago: University of Chicago Press, 2010.

Greene, Robert. *The Historie of Orlando Furioso, 1594.* Edited by W.W. Greg. London: The Malone Society, 1907.

Hazlitt, William. *Characters of Shakespear's Plays.* London: R. Hunter, 1817.

Harbage, Alfred. *Shakespeare: A Reader's Guide.* New York: Farrar, Strauss, and Co., 1963.

Hollyband, Claude. *A Dictionarie French and English.* London: Thomas Woodcock, 1593.

Howard, Jean. "Crossdressing, the Theatre, and Gender Struggle in Early Modern England." *Shakespeare Quarterly* 39 (1988): 418–40.

Huizinga, Johan. *Homo Ludens: A Study of the Play-Element in Culture.* London: Routledge, 2000.

Iser, Wolfgang. *The Fictive and the Imaginary: Charting Literary Anthropology.* Baltimore: Johns Hopkins University Press, 1993.

Jones, Ann Rosalind, and Peter Stallybrass. *Renaissance Clothing and the Materials of Memory.* Cambridge: Cambridge University Press, 2001.

Kermode, Frank. *The Sense of an Ending: Studies in the Theory of Fiction.* Oxford: Oxford University Press, 1968.

Knowles, Richard, ed. *A New Variorum Edition of* As You Like It. New York: Modern Language Association, 1977.

Kott, Jan. *Shakespeare Our Contemporary.* New York: W.W. Norton, 1974.

Lodge, Thomas. *Rosalynde.* Edited by Donald Beecher. Ottawa: Dovehouse Editions, 1997.

Marlowe, Christopher. *Dido Queen of Carthage.* Edited by Roma Gill. Vol. 1 of *The Complete Works: Translations: All Ovids Elegies, Lucans First Booke, Dido Queene of Carthage and Hero and Leander.* Oxford: Clarendon Press, 1987.

Masten, Jeffrey. "Textual Deviance: Ganymede's Hand in *As You Like It.*" In *Field Work: Sites in Literary and Cultural Studies,* edited by Marjorie Garber, Paul B. Franklin, and Rebecca L. Walkowitz, 153–63. New York: Routledge, 1996.

Mentz, Steve. "Shakespeare's Beach House, or, the Green and the Blue in *Macbeth.*" *Shakespeare Studies* 39 (2011): 84–93.

Middleton, Thomas. *Father Hubburd's Tales.* Edited by Adrian Weiss. In *The Collected Works,* general editors Gary Taylor and John Lavagnino, 164–82. Oxford: Clarendon Press, 2007.

Middleton, Thomas, and Thomas Dekker. *The Roaring Girle.* Edited by Coppélia Kahn. In *The Collected Works,* general editors Gary Taylor and John Lavagnino, 721–78. Oxford: Clarendon Press, 2007.

Montaigne, Michel Eyquem de. *Essais.* Edited by Pierre Villey. Paris: Presses Universitaires de France, 1965.

Nagel, Thomas. "What Is It Like To Be a Bat?" *The Philosophical Review* 83 (1974): 435–50.

Orgel, Stephen. *Impersonations: The Performance of Gender in Shakespeare's England.* Cambridge: Cambridge University Press, 1996.

Orgel, Stephen. "Nobody's Perfect: Or, Why Did the English Stage Take Boys for Women?" *South Atlantic Quarterly* 88 (1989): 7–29.

Piaget, Jean. *Play, Dreams and Imitation in Childhood.* Translated by C. Gattegne and F.M. Hodgson. New York: W.W. Norton, 1951.

Rackin, Phyllis. "Androgyny, Mimesis, and the Marriage of the Boy Heroine on the English Renaissance Stage." *PMLA* 102 (1987): 29–41.

Rackin, Phyllis. "Shakespeare's Crossdressing Comedies." In *A Companion to Shakespeare's Works: Literature and Culture*, Vol. 3, edited by Richard Dutton and Jean Howard. Oxford: Blackwell, 2003.

Rider, John. *Bibliotheca Scholastica*. Oxford: Joseph Barnes, 1589.

Shakespeare, William. *As You Like It*. Edited by Juliet Dusinberre. London: Bloomsbury, 2006.

Shakespeare, William. *Hamlet*. Edited by Ann Thompson and Neil Taylor. London: Bloomsbury, 2006.

Shakespeare, William. *Hamlet: The Texts of 1603 and 1623*. Edited by Ann Thompson and Neil Taylor. London: Bloomsbury, 2006.

Shakespeare, William. *King Lear*. Edited by R.A. Foakes. Walton-on-Thames: Arden, 1997.

Shakespeare, William. *Macbeth*. Edited by Frank Kermode. In *The Riverside Shakespeare*. Boston: Houghton Mifflin Co., 1997.

Shakespeare, William. *The Merchant of Venice*. Edited by John Drakakis. London: Arden, 2010.

Shapiro, Michael. *Gender in Play on the Shakespearean Stage: Boy Pages and Female Heroines*. Ann Arbor: University of Michigan Press, 1994.

Schiller, Friedrich. *On the Aesthetic Education of Man, in a Series of Letters*. Translated by Elizabeth M. Wilkinson. Oxford: Oxford University Press, 1986.

Schlegel, August. *A Course of Lectures on Dramatic Art and Literature*. 2 vols. Translated by John Black. London: Baldwin, Craddock, and Joy, 1815.

Shaw, George Bernard. *Shaw on Shakespeare: An Anthology of Bernard Shaw's Writings on the Plays and Production of Shakespeare*. 1961. Edited by Edwin Wilson. New York: Applause Books, 1989.

Smith, Bruce. *Phenomenal Shakespeare*. Chichester: Wiley-Blackwell, 2010.

Spenser, Edmund. *The Shepherd's Calendar*. 1579. In *The Shorter Poems of Edmund Spenser*, edited by William Oram et al. New Haven: Yale University Press, 1989.

Stauffer, Donald A. *Shakespeare's World of Images: The Development of His Moral Ideas*. New York: W.W. Norton, 1949.

Stern, Tiffany. "Was *Totus Mundus Agit Histrionem* ever the Motto of the Globe Theatre?" *Theatre Notebook* 51 (1997): 122–27.

Vaihinger, Hans. *The Philosophy of As-If*. 1911. Translated by C.K. Ogden. London: Routledge and Kegan Paul, 1924.

Van Doren, Mark. *Shakespeare*. New York: H. Holt, 1939.

Watson, Robert. *Back to Nature: The Green and the Real in the Late Renaissance*. Philadelphia: University of Pennsylvania Press, 2006.

Winnicott, D.W. *Playing and Reality*. 1971. New York: Routledge, 1989.

Wittgenstein, Ludwig. *Culture and Value*. Translated by Peter Winch. Chicago: University of Chicago Press, 1980.

Worde, Wynkyn de. *Ortus Vocabulorum*. London: Wynkyn de Worde, 1500.

W. dreams, like Phaedrus, of an army of thinker-friends, thinker-lovers. He dreams of a thought-army, a thought-pack, which would storm the philosophical Houses of Parliament. He dreams of Tartars from the philosophical steppes, of thought-barbarians, thought-outsiders. What distance would shine in their eyes!

— Lars Iyer

www.ingramcontent.com/pod-product-compliance
Lightning Source LLC
Chambersburg PA
CBHW051131160426
43195CB00014B/2435